Garfield Robinson

DARE TO CONTEND

A DEFENSE OF THE DOCTRINE OF SALVATION

Extra MILE Innovators
Kingston, Jamaica, W.I.

Copyright © 2022 by Garfield Robinson
ISBN: 978-976-96863-5-9

ALL RIGHTS RESERVED

Without limiting the rights under copyright reserved above, no part of this publication may be reproduced, stored in or introduced into a retrieval system, or transmitted, in any form, or by any means (electronic, mechanical, photocopying, recording, or otherwise), without the prior contractual or written permission of the copyright owner of this work.

First printed: June 2022

Published by:
Extra MILE Innovators
4 Rochester Avenue,
Kingston 8, Jamaica W.I.
www.extramileja.com

Cover Design: Albert Burkett
origmullob@yahoo.com

Formatting: BambuSparks | www.bambusparks.com

Unless otherwise noted all Scripture quotations are taken from the New International Version (NIV) from the Holy Bible, New International Version; copyright © 1973, 1978, 1984, 2010 by the International Bible Society, and Biblica, Inc.™ Used by permission. All rights reserved worldwide.

Author Contact: For consultation, feedback or speaking engagements, contact the author at robinsongarfield15@gmail.com.

To all those who have devoted themselves to rightly dividing the word of God and contending for the body of pure doctrine that has been passed down to us.

Acknowledgments

I want to thank the people who have helped in completing this project: to Aretha Willie, Inez Small and Dawitt Ming, for their patient labour in proofreading the manuscript. Thank you!

I also want to thank Dr. Dylan Toussaint for interacting with the manuscript and endorsing it. Finally, I wish to thank Ruth Taylor for her wisdom and guidance, and my publisher, Extra MILE Innovators for the wonderful work they have done. This project could not be a success without them.

Foreword

Those who have read Garfield Robinson's book *Dare to Ask* will attest to the fact that he has a *penchant* for simplifying Bible-related issues which may be considered complex and even controversial.

It should, therefore, come as no surprise that in this his more recent publication 'Dare to Contend', Robinson daringly tackles head-on some of the most challenging concepts and concerns, albeit from Biblical and Theological perspectives, guided by the timely and timeless principles of hermeneutics.

In so doing, questions and answers in relation to topics such as: Salvation, Justification, Regeneration, Sanctification, Redemption, Reconciliation, Predestination and Election, *inter alia*, are addressed in the book.

The title is, obviously and undoubtedly, influenced by Jude 3 which states: "Beloved, when I gave all diligence to write unto you of the common salvation, it was needful of me to write unto you and exhort you that ye should earnestly **contend** for the faith which was once delivered unto the saints" (KJV).

However, Garfield gives an innovative and interesting twist to the word 'Contend' by using an acronym to highlight his intended and suggested approach to the selected-topics and subsequent-tasks.

The result is a reader-friendly and user-friendly document which may serve as a reference book, inclusive of additional pertinent and provocative questions for personal contemplation and/or public discussion. Either way, those who open-mindedly and analytically explore its contents should be better equipped to "Contend for the Faith" and thus actualize the words of Peter, "But in your hearts revere Christ as Lord. Always be prepared to give an answer to everyone who asks you to give the reason for the hope that you have..." (I Peter 3: 15, NIV).

Rev. Dr. Dylan Toussaint
Pastor, Edgewater/Waterford
Circuit of Baptist Churches
Former Adjunct Lecturer,
Jamaica Theological Seminary

Introduction

The Zealous Man Who Got Beat Up

One day while watching a fight on the road, I took notice of the man who was losing. He seemed passionate, well-motivated and had powerful punches, but he lacked tactics and practice. His opponent was just picking him apart in the fight, using good tactics and timing. It became clear to me that day that a person needs more than just passion to win a fight.

As I considered the battle we are in as Christians, I realized that the same is true for us, because passion alone will not do. We have a responsibility to contend for the faith, or the body of doctrine which has been passed on to us; but more importantly, we need to know why we ought to contend, and how to do it. If we are going to do well at contending for the truth of God's word, then we need to know the truth for ourselves.

I will attempt to clarify what I mean by contend, by using an acronym to explain what the task is.

The letter **C** in "CONTEND" stands for to combat or to compete against. It carries the idea of resisting or going against something. In this case, for the purpose of this book, we are pushing against the false doctrines that seek to cripple believers in their faith; and against the obstacles which stand in the way of those who want to come to faith in Jesus. Jude 1:3 exhorts us also, to withstand and compete against false teaching. The Apostle Paul had to stand against Peter whose behavior, in one instance, was sending a wrong message and distorting the truth (Galatians 2:11-14). Part of the process of contending is correcting and rebuking those who misrepresent the Scriptures.

The letter **O** highlights the need for Obedience. This means that if we are to carry out this task of contending, we need to obey God's instructions. We are called to comply and to adhere to His Words (Col. 2:6-8). The **N** refers to Nullify. This is when we demonstrate that their teaching is useless and erroneous. For example, the Apostle Paul in 1 Corinthians 15 gave arguments in defense of the resurrection. He pointed how meaningless and hopeless life is without the resurrection. This is so because if there is no resurrection, then Christ is not risen, their preaching is vain, and their faith is also meaningless.

The **T** points to Teach. We have a responsibility to educate people about what the Scriptures say, and what the Scriptures mean. The Apostle Paul demonstrated this responsibility when he opposed some people who were teaching false doctrine in the church at Corinth, and he explained to the believers that they ought to defend the faith and teach truth of God's Word (1 Timothy 4:1-6). We are also exhorted in 1Timothy 4:12 to be an example of the believers through a pure and Godly lifestyle; one which is guided by the Holy Spirit and Scripture.

We should use the Word of God as our primary and final authority because it is useful for doctrine, instruction, correction, and encouragement, for this is the only way people will come to maturity in Christ (2 Timothy 3:16-17). If we are willing to study to show ourselves approved unto God as we are commanded to in 2 Timothy 2:15, we will be able to rightly divide the word to the benefit of others and to ourselves.

The **E** in the acronym invites us to Examine the Word. That is extremely important because we need to evaluate very carefully whatever we read or hear. The **N** represents to Nurture. As we saw in our reference above, the word rightly taught, is what will bring people to maturity as we seek to nurture them with the milk and the meat of the Word of God (1 Peter 2:2). Therefore, in the same way we care for a newborn baby by feeding and nurturing until the child is taught how to feed him or herself, we must do the same for the new converts.

The **D** stands for Demolish. This refers to the act of tearing down every argument that is raised up against the truth of Scripture. 2 Corinthians 10:5 says, we must pull down everything that exalts itself above the knowledge of Christ. There are some persons in church who like to have their own way because of personal preferences. They will insist that others submit to their ideas even when it conflicts with Scripture, which is our primary authority. We must not give room to this attitude inside the church or inside our minds. I hope you are ready to contend for the faith.

Let's go to war!

Contents

Acknowledgements v

Foreword vii

Introduction ix

CHAPTER 1. Salvation 1

    1.1 How It Started for Me 2

    1.2 Start with the Bible 3

    Recommended Reading 7

    1.3 What is the Plan of Salvation? 8

    1.4 The Person Who Saves 10

CHAPTER 2. Justification 15

    2.1 The Meaning of Justification 16

    2.2 The Method of Justification 17

CHAPTER 3. Regeneration 21

    3.1. The Meaning of Regeneration 22

    3.2 The Method of Regeneration 22

CHAPTER 4. Total Depravity 31
    4.1 What is Total Depravity? 32

CHAPTER 5. Irresistible Grace 47
    5.1 What is Irresistible Grace? 48

CHAPTER 6. Sanctification 51
    6.1 The Concept of Sanctification 52
    6.2 The Contents of Sanctification 52
    6.3 The Command to Sanctification 53
    6.4 The Comfort of Sanctification 56

CHAPTER 7. Redemption 59
    7.1. What is Redemption? 60
    7.2. The Practice of Redemption 62
    7.3. The Person of Redemption 62
    7.4. The Price of Redemption 63
    7.5. The Purchase of Redemption 64
    7.6. The Period of Redemption 65
    7.7. The Product of Redemption 66
    7.8. The Planet was Redeemed 67
    7.9 The Plan of Redemption 72

CHAPTER 8. Reconciliation 77
    8.1 What is Reconciliation? 78
    8.2 The Reason for Reconciliation 79
    8.3 The Reach of Reconciliation 80

8.4 The Response to Reconciliation 80

8.5 The Result of Reconciliation 81

CHAPTER 9. Predestination 85

9.1 What is Predestination? 86

CHAPTER 10 Election 93

10.1. What is the Meaning of Election? 94

10.2. God's Choice of the Boys 96

10.3. God's Choice of Pharaoh 99

10.4. How Does One Get Saved? 110

10.5. How Does Election Work? 116

10.6. What are they Chosen to do? 121

CHAPTER 11: God's Sovereignty 125

11.1. What is the Meaning of Sovereignty? 126

11.2. The Manifestation of God's Sovereignty 127

CHAPTER 12. Compatibilism? 131

12.1. What is Compatibilism? 132

12.2. Is Compatibilism Supported by the Bible? 134

12.3. Making it Plain: Determinism laid bare 145

CHAPTER 13. The Love of God 157

13.1. God: The Lover 158

13.2. Is this Love? 161

CHAPTER 14. Amazing Grace 165

14. 1. What is Grace? 166
14.2. The Good News of Grace.. 168
14.3. Grace to Enter 168
15.4. Grace to Enable 169
14.5. Don't take Grace for Granted 170
14. 6. Grace to Engage 171
14. 7. Grace to Endure 173
14.8. Grace to End Well 174

Conclusion 176
References 179

CHAPTER 1

Salvation

I.I
How It Started for Me

Have you ever heard a message that you could not get out of your mind? One evening, a pastor came and shared the Gospel with a group of young people talking about sports. After he spoke, none of us openly accepted the Lord that evening, as far as I know. However, while I was in my bed that night, I could not get the message out of my mind. I took up my Bible and opened it to a passage that said, "For what shall it profit a man if he gains the whole world and lose his soul? Or what shall a man give in exchange for his soul?" (Mark 8:36-37, KJV). I immediately slammed the Bible shut because I did not want to deal with that question. To me, it felt like an interrogation. I could hear the Lord asking me, "What does it profit me if I get all the fame and all the wealth, and I lose my soul in the end"? When I thought about all that God had done for me, I accepted the gracious gift of God; his offer of salvation to save my soul as I trusted in Christ for salvation that night.

From then on, I have always had a deep desire to study what the Bible has to say about salvation. I have sought to get a good grasp of this particular subject for over 25 years. At my church, the inductive method of studying the Bible was taught, and I have sought to use it ever since. This helped me to contend with some of the materials that were taught while I was a student Seminary. I believe some of the materials I read grossly misrepresented the character and love of God, and I was only able to contend with those materials because I was already armed with the skills of rightly dividing the Word of Truth (the Bible).

I am convinced that students of the Bible need to be taught how to do effective Bible study (hermeneutics), before they are taught systematic theology. If the students don't learn how to study the Scriptures for themselves, they won't be able to tell whether or not the teacher is correctly representing the Bible. We need to develop the Berean approach where, after the Apostle Paul had finished teaching, the believers went back to search the Scriptures for themselves to verify if what he said was true (Acts 17:11). They wanted to make sure that Paul's teaching corresponded with the Word of God.

1.2 Start with the Bible

The Bible is such a fascinating and intriguing book that it has caused people to cling to it for centuries. In all generations and for many people, the Bible has been that source of comfort and direction while navigating the experiences in life. The primary benefit is the great salvation that has been offered to the world. The main topic will be the salvation that God has provided.

As we delve into the study of this interesting topic of the great salvation that God has provided through Jesus Christ, I want everyone to understand what the Scriptures say about salvation. If we are going to accomplish that, we must have a good understanding of the basic principles of effective Bible Study. In my opinion, the most basic and best approach to effective Bible Study is the Inductive Method. This approach to Bible Study has three sections. Firstly, the Observation Section that asks the question, "What do I see?" Secondly, the Interpretation Section which asks the question, "What does this mean?" And thirdly, the Application Section which asks the question, "How does this apply to me today?" Please note that these are investigative questions which will help us to collect information from the text.

Since our study is on this very important, but sometimes very controversial topic, I want us to take some time just to pause and lay aside our assumptions and presuppositions so that we can look at the Scriptures afresh and see what the Scriptures actually say. This is important because we all come to the Bible with some assumptions and presuppositions that we may have held for a long time and, therefore, it becomes difficult for us to see differently and embrace what is actually there in the text. Let us first rid ourselves of those.

As we seek to understand what the author is trying to communicate to his reader, the first thing we need to do is note what the passage says. Do not read any former view or understanding into the text. At this point you are only concerned with what the text says. Ask questions of the text such as, who is speaking? To whom is he or she speaking? What did he or she say? Where did it happen? When did it happen? Was it before the Resurrection or Pentecost? These preliminary questions can help you to reap valuable information that will certainly aid in your interpretation.

Your observation needs to also take note of the genre that you are reading, so that you don't come away with a flawed interpretation of the text. For example, find out if what you are reading is a parable, a proverb, or poetry. This is important because all genres are not interpreted the same way. We have to understand how to treat the text that uses figurative languages and idioms. For example, when someone says that it is raining cats and dogs, we don't look outside to see cats and dogs falling from the sky. The person is simply saying that it is raining heavily. If I say that I am going to let the cat out of the bag, it is the culture and context of my conversation that will let you know whether I am going to release a four-legged animal, or I am about to reveal a secret.

Context is king when seeking to understand Scripture. So, we need to check to see if the passage is using parabolic language, or describing a vision, or reporting a literal historical event. This will help us to arrive at the correct meaning of the text. Remember not to get too caught up with endless word studies. Although it is important to understand the word in its root form, the meaning of the word will ultimately be determined by its context. In the process of biblical interpretation, the key is the context. A word should be understood by the context in which it is used. Note the historical, cultural, and literary context.

We must not approach Scripture with an attitude of pride, as if we are the determiner of the meaning, but rather as seekers, who want to discover the intended meaning of the author. Being able to read Greek is not the same as being able to do good exegesis. A person may be able to read the language of the text and still miss the true meaning of the text. Flawed interpretation can be done whether one knows Greek, Spanish, French, or English.

While you take this journey into Scripture, I want to give you the primary message of the Bible up front. According to John 5:39 Jesus said, "You diligently study the Scriptures because you think that by them you possess eternal life. These are the Scriptures that testify about me." Luke 24:27 also tells us that Jesus, while on the road to Emmaus with the two disciples, explained to them, beginning with Moses and all the prophets all the Scriptures said concerning Himself. Jesus came to pay for the sins of the world, and He also came to give the right picture of what the Heavenly Father is like (John 1:18, Hebrews 1:1-3). Therefore, the main message of the Bible is that Jesus is the Saviour who came to redeem mankind through faith in His Name; and to show the world what the Father is like.

Jesus bought and offered this Great Salvation to us. We will do well to embrace it; for how shall we escape judgment if we neglect such a Great Salvation (Hebrews 2:3). I will attempt to deal with salvation on a whole and try to clarify the meanings of the components of salvation. These include doctrines such as Reconciliation, Justification, Redemption, Sanctification, Regeneration, Adoption, Election, Predestination, and the wonderful Amazing Grace of God.

I, primarily take a Bible study approach to the topic of salvation as I contend for the faith. It could be described as a Berean approach of searching the Scriptures. This work is not an attempt to present the perspectives of theological scholars on this subject. Here is a list of books that I will recommend if you want a deeper dive into the study of the doctrine of salvation.

Recommended Reading

Allan, David. *The Extent of the Atonement: A Historical and Critical Review*. Nashville Band H Academic, 2016.

Flowers, Leighton. *The Potter's Promise: A Defense of Traditional Soteriology*. Trinity Academic, 2017.

Lennox, John C. Determined to Believe? *The Sovereignty of God, Freedom, Faith, and Human Responsibility*. Grand Rapids: Zondervan, 2017

Rogers, Ronnie W. *Does God Love All or Some? Comparing Biblical Extensivism and Calvinism's Exclusivism*. Wipf and Stock Publishers, 2019

1.3
What is the Plan of Salvation?

The plan of salvation was in the Mind of God before human beings were even created. God is an Eternal Being who exists outside of time, and He has all knowledge of all events. Even events that will happen in the future are in the present for Him, because he is not looking down the corridors of time to know things. All of time is presently in front of Him, and He can see it as an individual looking down at a ball on the floor. So, although we have experienced events in the past and also look to the future events, all events come into being in time, but God exists (was and is still) outside of time.

Through His omniscience (all knowledge), God was aware of all that mankind would do when given the ability to choose to obey or to rebel. So, God made a plan to redeem mankind because He knew that mankind was going to fail and fall in the garden. God was not the one who caused mankind to sin. Mankind sinned when they were tempted by the devil (Genesis 3:1-7). God cannot be tempted with evil; therefore, He doesn't tempt anyone to sin. As a matter of fact, James says that one sins when one is drawn away by one's own lust and enticed (James 1:13-14).

The need for salvation was occasioned when mankind sinned in the Garden of Eden, and from that point forward, was separated from the life and intimacy that was had with God. Mankind was judged by God because of their transgression, and became dead in their trespass and sin. Remember, God told Adam and Eve that they will die if they eat of the forbidden fruit (Genesis 2:17).

Nevertheless, they took their chances and disobeyed God's command. Eve listened to the devil who told her she will not surely die; but they surely did. They did not die physically that day, but the curse of death was on them from that day. They began to die physically, but they were immediately cut off from the intimacy they had with God which is the spiritual death. Death in Scripture speaks to separation. For example, the spirit separated from the body is death; the person separated from God is death, and faith separated from corresponding action is dead.

There was an instant death in the souls of Adam and Eve that rendered them as aliens instead of friends and family of God. God also cast them outside of the Garden so that they will not eat of the fruit of the Tree of Life and live forever in their sinful and separated state (Gen. 3:22-24). God wants us to not just exist but to have the quality of eternal life with Him.

There was now a need for salvation because they had become sinners, and come short of the glory of God. So, mankind needed two things to be set right with God. These two things are forgiveness and glory. The problem for mankind was not just about receiving forgiveness from God, because they had lost a state of glory that they enjoyed in the presence of God, before they disobeyed. The sin of Adam and Eve rendered them unfit to fellowship with God as before, because they were now unholy beings. Lucifer also lost his privileges when he sinned and was thrown out of heaven. Sin has brought about disapproval and rejection from God because mankind was no longer seen as good, as in the state they were created (Genesis 1:31). Therefore, we will only be able to stand in the presence of the Holy God when we are clothed in Christ's righteousness and share in His glory. Therefore, we needed a righteousness which comes only through faith in God. According to 2 Corinthians 5:21, we are the righteousness of God in Christ. We who share in this life with Christ, will also share in His glory, and we will be glorified together (Romans 8:17). God deals with the sin and the status, so that those who trust in Christ can have life through Him.

1.4
The Person Who Saves

Jesus is the Person Who saves; apart from Him there is no Saviour. Acts 4:12 says "Salvation is found in no one else, for there is no other name under heaven given to mankind by which we must be saved." It was already prophesied in Genesis that the Seed of the woman will crush the head of the serpent (Genesis 3:18). This was fulfilled at Calvary when Jesus died on the cross. The enemy thought they had won, but Christ's death was the very means of victory. He triumphed over them when He rose for our justification (Romans 4:25). The means of accomplishing salvation was hidden from the devil and his host of followers. 1 Corinthians 2:8 tells us that "None of the rulers of this age understood it, for if they had, they would not have crucified the Lord of Glory." Please note that we just mentioned that salvation was purchased by means of Jesus' death, burial, and resurrection, but the Gospel is the power of God unto salvation to everyone who believes (Romans 1:16).

Now, there are different aspects of salvation. For example, when we read the Scriptures carefully, we will realize that sometimes the text is referring to temporal salvation, which is another word for deliverance. Many times, the people of God are said to be saved or delivered, and this is talking about being protected or rescued by God from their enemies. So, we need to note in the context if it is referring to eternal salvation of the soul, or just being saved from a situation. An example of this was demonstrated at Calvary where we see two thieves being crucified to the left and right side of Jesus. One wanted to be delivered from his temporary situation, while the other wanted eternal deliverance from his sin (Luke 23:39-44).

There are other examples in the Bible. In Exodus 14:13 we read "... stand firm and you will see the deliverance the Lord will bring you today ...." 2 Chronicles 20:17 makes a similar point about God delivering His people from the enemy or persecution. At other times the Bible speaks about deliverance from sin. In Luke 19:10 we are told that Jesus came to seek and to save the lost. Matthew 1:21 says that Jesus will save His people from their sins. In 1 Timothy 1:15, the Apostle Paul says that "Here is a trustworthy saying that deserves full acceptance: Christ Jesus came into the world to save sinners of whom I am the worst.

The Scriptures also present different states and stages of salvation. For example, it speaks of salvation as a past event, as a present event, and as a future event. We were saved the day we trusted in Jesus for salvation (Ephesians 1:12). Therefore, we were delivered from the penalty of sin. There is no condemnation to those who are in Christ (Romans 8:1). We have passed from death to life and will not come into condemnation (John 5:24). The Bible also makes it clear that we are being delivered from the power of sin that is in our members; the body (Roman 6:11-14). Since we are new creatures in Christ, we must not allow sin to reign in our bodies. We are new people who ought to demonstrate new practices in our lifestyle. This can only be accomplished as we rely on the Holy Spirit's power and guidance. The Apostle Paul says to us in Galatians 5:16, "So I say, walk by the Spirit and you will not gratify the desires of the flesh." That means if we keep in step with the Holy Spirit and are led by Him, we will not live in the flesh or fulfill its desires. There is also a future aspect of salvation. This speaks to the future event when everything will be made new, and the believers will be glorified when the fullness of their salvation has come.

Therefore, we still speak about our hope of salvation, which happens at the day of the redemption of the body (1 John 3:1-3). 1 Peter 1:5 mentions the salvation ready to be revealed. Also, in verse 9 it says that we will receive at the end of our faith, the salvation of our souls. The Apostle Paul tells us that now our salvation is nearer than when we first believed (Romans 13:11). This simply means that we are closer to that day when we will enjoy and experience the fullness of our salvation. There is greater joy awaiting us, because we are not yet what we shall be; better days are coming. Hallelujah!

So, we were saved from the penalty of sin in the past; we are being saved from the power of sin in our members, and also, in the world and against the devil. We will be saved from the very presence of sin in the future. The Bible speaks of a day when there will be no more crying, no more dying, no more pain or shame, because all will be made new (Revelation 21:4-5). The people who will enjoy this Great Salvation are those who recognize that they are sinners, and therefore, they cannot save themselves. They are the people who have trusted in Jesus as their personal Lord and Savior; those who, in humility, have laid aside their own righteousness, which is as filthy rags before God, and have received the righteousness of Christ by faith.

Questions to Contemplate/Discuss

A. What is Salvation?
B. Why was Salvation necessary?
C. Who are the persons that are saved?
D. What are the different types of Salvation?
E. The Gospel is the power of God unto Salvation to whom?

CHAPTER 2

Justification

2.1
The Meaning of Justification

Justification deals with our past, present, and future status of righteousness before God. Please note that Justification is not regeneration. Regeneration speaks to one being born again by the Spirit of God. The topic and definition of regeneration will be discussed later. What I want to make clear though, is that justification is not what gives us a new life; that is accomplished at conversion through regeneration. Justification gives us a new status or standing before God. We are no longer considered to be sinful enemies, but rather we are righteous friends in the family of God through Jesus Christ our Lord.

Justification goes beyond being forgiven. Forgiveness is important because it releases us from our sin debt. However, we needed more than pardon. We needed a righteousness that is perfect before God that causes us to be accepted in His presence. This we cannot accomplish of ourselves, so we receive it by faith in Jesus Christ. When God imputes righteousness to our account, we now have a status as if we have never sinned. Please don't misunderstand what I'm saying here. I am not implying that we are not sinful and wretched. What I am saying is that Christ's righteousness has been placed on the believer's account; so that Christ's righteousness is what the Father sees when He looks at them.

2.2
The Method of Justification

Justification is a key component in salvation. It is the means by which a sinner is declared righteous when he puts his faith in Christ for salvation. In Christianity, justification takes place when God puts a righteous standing on a sinner's account; one who has trusted in Jesus. So, God gives the person a new legal position before Him. There is only one way a person can be justified before God, and that is by faith. We read in Romans 5:1, "Therefore, since we have been justified through faith, we have peace with God through our Lord Jesus Christ." The following verse states that we have access by faith into this grace in which we stand. Jesus' shed blood is used as a means to our justification (Romans 5:9), and His resurrection seals it (Romans 4:25). This is how we were put back into right standing with God

No one is justified before God by the deeds of the law (Romans 3:20). Individuals cannot do enough good deeds to be justified in God's sight. Therefore, they must humble themselves before God and trust in God's provision of righteousness. James 4:6 says that God resists the proud, but gives grace to the humble. It is God who justifies. The Apostle Paul states in Galatians 2:16, "Know that a person is not justified by the works of the law, but by faith in Christ Jesus that we may be justified by faith in Christ and not by the works of the law, because by the works of the law no one will be justified." The way this works, is that if you try to earn it, you won't get it, but if you rely on and rest in God's provision of righteousness, you will receive it.

In Romans 3:24 the Apostle Paul says, "... all are justified freely by His grace through the redemption that came by Christ

Jesus." Therefore, he concluded that a man is justified by faith without the deeds of the law (Romans 3:28). Romans 10:4 says that "Christ is the culmination of the law so that there may be righteousness for everyone who believes."

Therefore, faith in Christ is essential for the application of justification. Genesis 15:6 says that Abraham believed in God, and it was counted to him for righteousness. This truth is also repeated in Romans 4:3. In Romans 10:10 we are told, "For it is with your heart that you believe and are justified, and it is with your mouth that you profess your faith and are saved." Titus 3:7 says, "So that, having been justified by His grace, we might become heirs having the hope of eternal life."

According to the Apostle Paul in Galatians 3:8, God preached the Gospel to Abraham, saying that the nations will be blessed through him. God justified the people through faith. Therefore, no one has the right to condemn those whom God has justified. Tony Evans (1999), speaking on the impact of what happens in justification says, "the reason we have peace with God once we have been justified is that neither Satan nor anyone else can ever go back and bring up those sins against us." Evans went on to make the point that "Jesus is our Advocate or Attorney who stands in the gap for us."

Here, Evans agrees with the Apostle Paul who says, ". . . If God be for us who can be against us?" (Romans 8:31). "Who will bring any charge against those whom God has chosen? It is God who justifies" (Romans 8:33). This truth is also found in 1 John 2:1. If we are justified, we must live by faith. James says that the only way someone can see your faith is if it has corresponding actions. Otherwise, it is just a "say faith," which can be regarded as head knowledge. James pointed out how Abraham demonstrated his faith by what he did (James 2:21, 24-25). He is not claiming that Abraham was justified or declared righteous before God by his works, because long before he offered Isaac to God, God imputed righteousness to him because he believed in God (Genesis 15:6). The point is that the just must live by faith (Romans1:17, Galatians 3:11). So, if you believe, let it show through your actions.

Questions to Contemplate / Discuss

    a. What is Justification?
    b. Who are justified?
    c. How are they justified?
    d. How is Justification different from Regeneration?
    e. What role does Justification play in salvation?

CHAPTER 3
Regeneration

3.1.
The Meaning of Regeneration

Regeneration is a very important component in salvation that we need to understand. We all need to begin with a clear understanding of what the Bible says about regeneration. Let me begin with a definition of regeneration. Regeneration takes place when the Holy Spirit gives new spiritual life to someone who puts his / her faith in Jesus Christ for salvation. Regeneration is also described as being born from above (John 1: 13), and being born again (John 3:3). The Holy Spirit also seals us (Ephesians 1:13), and baptizes us in Christ's body (1 Corinthians 12:13). This is how God marks and secures those who belong to Him.

3.2
The Method of Regeneration

God uses a method to save people which includes them hearing the message and receiving the Gospel that brings salvation. We believe that salvation is totally of God, and we also believe in the means that God has chosen to bring regeneration.

The way it works is that God sends a messenger through various means to bring the Gospel to the unsaved person. The Holy Spirit then convicts the person of his sins, which leads him to a point of trusting in Christ and repenting of his sin. The Holy Spirit then takes that person, and places him into the Body of Christ. The Holy Spirit indwells him, which serves as a mark or seal that the person is now a child of God. Therefore, it is the convicting work of the Holy Spirit coupled with the surrender of the person in humility and trust in Jesus that causes a person to become a new creation in Christ. This does not mean that the person is "helping" God to save him/her; but it does mean receiving the gift of God through faith in Christ Jesus. God is the Person who offers salvation, but He is not the one who receives the salvation for me; I am the one who receives salvation.

Let us look at the Scriptural evidence for this. In the Bible regeneration comes after a person believes in Christ. It is when one accepts the message of the Gospel that one places one's faith in Christ and is born again. Since Adam sinned in the Garden of Eden, mankind lost their intimate position with God. God had promised them that in the day they sin, they will die (Genesis 2:17). Adam and Eve disobeyed God and the consequence of that was death. They did not immediately die physically, but eventually they did.

However, they immediately died spiritually. When I say that they died spiritually, I mean that they were separated from God and lost their intimate relationship with God. This changed something in their nature and their attitude towards God. Instead of enjoying the presence and fellowship with God, they were now running away, afraid and hiding from God (Genesis 3: 8-10).

The Apostle Paul while speaking with the saints of Ephesus stated, "As for you, you were dead in your transgressions and sins ..." (Ephesians 2:1). Later in the same chapter, he reminded the believers who, and where, they were before they trusted Christ for salvation. He said, "Remember that at that time you were separate from Christ, excluded from the citizenship in Israel and foreigners to the covenants of the promise, without hope and without God in the world. But now in Christ Jesus you who were far away, have been brought near by the blood of Christ" (Ephesians 2: 12 -13).

Notice that before they were saved and put into Christ, they were all outside of Christ and without hope, and without God in the world. The same author tells us how, and when, the Ephesians were saved. In chapter 1:13-14 he says,

> ..and you also were included in Christ when you heard the message of truth, the gospel of your salvation. When you believed, you were marked in Him with a seal, the promise Holy Spirit, who is a deposit, guaranteeing our inheritance until the redemption of those who are God's possessions to the praise of His glory (Ephesians 1:13-14).

The Holy Spirit seals the believer after he has placed his faith in Christ. Those who trust Christ have been sealed (Ephesians 4:30)

The person, who confesses Jesus Christ as Lord, and believes from the heart that God has raised Jesus from the dead, shall be saved. For with the heart a man believes and is made righteous, and with the mouth he confesses and is saved (Romans 10:9-10). There are some persons today teaching the opposite of what the Apostle Paul says here and in many other places. They insist that a person is regenerated before he believed the Gospel and trust in Christ; however, that is not supported by the Scripture.

A careful reading of Scripture will reveal that regeneration always come after faith, and never before faith. In John 1:11-12, we read 'He came to that which was His own, but his own did not receive him. Yet to all who did receive Him, to those who BELIEVE on His name, He gave the right to become children of

God." It is clear that the right to become a child of God is only given to those people who believe in Christ, and receive Him as Saviour. The Apostle Paul tells us in Romans 1:16 that the Gospel is the power of God unto salvation to everyone who believes. Please note that he did not say the power of God unto salvation to whom He chooses, but to everyone who BELIEVES. In 1 Corinthians 1:21, we are told that it pleased God to use preaching to save those who BELIEVE. Note again that the life or regeneration always come after faith is applied.

Eternal life is a gift, but it must be received for someone to benefit from its goodness. Faith comes by hearing the Word of God (Romans 10:17). However, just hearing the Gospel is not sufficient for someone to receive new life of the Spirit; you must receive the gift. God is not rendered any less kind when people reject His gift; they, however, are poorer for their rejection of the offer. James 1:18 says, "He chose to give us birth through the Word of Truth, that we might be a kind of first fruits of all He created."

The Word of God is the means that the Spirit of God uses to convict and convince persons to trust in Jesus. Hebrews 4:12 says, "For the Word of God is alive and active. Sharper than any double-edged sword, it penetrates even to dividing soul and spirit, joints and marrow; it judges the thoughts and attitudes of the heart." The powerful Word of God is potent enough to accomplish what God sent it to do. In the New Testament, the verse that actually mentions regeneration as it pertains to salvation is Titus 3:5. Let us look at what the Apostle Paul says, "He saved us, not because of righteous things we have done, but because of His mercy. He saved us through the washing of rebirth and renewal by the Holy Spirit." So, the Holy Spirit is the One who brings renewal by imparting new life to the person.

Those, therefore, who insist that regeneration precedes faith, are obviously not aware that regeneration is a New Testament component. This is important to note because many people were saved in the Old Testament, but they were not indwelt by the Holy Spirit. For example, Abraham believed God and it was accounted to him as righteousness (Genesis 15:16). That means God credited Abraham with righteousness because he believed in God (Romans 4:3). David, Moses, Joshua, Elijah, and many other Old Testament saints were saved, but they were not regenerated or indwelt by the Holy Spirit. They were not indwelt by the Holy Spirit because the Holy Spirit had not yet come to indwell believers. John 7:38-39 says that the Holy Spirit was not yet given. So, although the Holy Spirit would empower believers for the task at hand, and although He was actively involved in the world from the creation (Genesis 1:2), He was not residing in anyone.

This truth is confirmed by Jesus in John 14:15-17 where He told His disciples that He was going to send the Holy Spirit; and the Spirit is coming to indwell them or to live inside of them. Notice that all these disciples and the Old Testament saints were able to believe and be saved even though they had not been regenerated. They were given right standing with God because of their faith in God. In John 20:30-31 we read, "Jesus performs many other signs in the presence of His disciples, which are not recorded in this book. But these are written that you may believe that Jesus is the Messiah, the Son of God, and that by believing you may have life in His name." Notice who will get this new life, this regeneration; it is those who BELIEVE. The purpose for the writing of the Word is so that people might BELIEVE and have life.

The same Apostle John says something similar in 1 John 5:10-13, "Whoever believes in the Son of God accepts this testimony. Whoever does not believe God has made Him out to be a liar, because they have not believed the testimony God has given of His Son. And this is the testimony: God has given us eternal life, and this life is in His Son. Whoever has the Son has life; whoever does not have the Son of God does not have life. I write these things to you who believe in the name of the Son of God so that you may know that you have eternal life."

In the references above and those to follow, what we will see is that regeneration always comes after one believes. This is how the new life is given. This is how eternal life is received, through faith. Paul the Apostle tells us in Galatians 3:26, "So in Christ you are all children of God through faith." Over and over again we see this truth in the pages of Scripture. Remember faith comes by hearing the life giving, powerful, and soul piercing Word of God. We are saved by grace through faith, according to Ephesians 2:8. It goes on to tell us that salvation is a gift of God, which we cannot earn by our good works, so no one has a right to boast (Ephesians 2:9).

A key component in salvation is justification. By that I mean to be declared righteous in Christ. This is done when the person trusts in Christ, as we find in Romans 3:26-28. It says,

> He did it to demonstrate His righteousness, at the present time, so as to be just and the one who justifies those who have faith in Jesus. Where, then is boastings? It is excluded. Because of what law? The law that requires works? No, because of the law that requires faith. For we maintain that a person is justified by faith apart from the works of the law.

So, it is evident that the people who are made righteous are those who believe. Faith is constantly contrasted with the works of the Law in the Apostle Paul's letters (Galatians 3:21-29, Romans 10:4). Therefore, those who try to define or describe faith in Jesus Christ as a work that someone does that earn their way to God, are just being deceitful or ignorant about what the Bible says about faith in Christ. The Scriptures contrast faith with the works of the Law.

Some push their doctrine that regeneration precedes faith, but they are not using the term regeneration the way the Bible uses it. If these persons know what regeneration means in scripture, I think that they are being disingenuous by insisting on putting a different meaning to it in order to support their worldview. When a person hears the Gospel, is he regenerated then? Not according to Scripture, as I have demonstrated through the evidence in the Bible. If the Holy Spirit regenerates a person before he hears the Gospel, is the Gospel still the power of God unto salvation, even though he has not believed. This is a clear twisting of the Scripture. Not only that, but they insist that if someone hears the Gospel and trusts in Christ, the individual is helping God in his salvation.

The person who preaches the Gospel to the individual, is he also helping God to save the individual? Should the Evangelist get some of the glory since God spoke through him? By no means! Salvation is of God alone, and He uses the powerful life-changing, life-giving Word of God to pierce the heart because it is sufficient for someone to believe. How could it be said that when the Holy Spirit uses the Word to convict the heart of a man and he believes in God, he is working for his salvation? Isn't all the means that God uses sufficient to accomplish His will? Does the preacher also participate in the saving of the person, or is it still true that God is the only Savior? I hope they can see the conflict or contradiction in their teaching. Since they are not prepared to give some of the glory of salvation to the preacher, they must stop claiming that the sinner gets glory for his salvation when he believes. The Word of God is spirit and life (John 6: 63).

So, if you ask me how a person is regenerated, I can tell you what the Scripture plainly says. Receive Jesus as your Lord and Saviour; believe in His work on the cross on your behalf, and the Holy Spirit will regenerate or give you eternal life. If you believe on the Lord Jesus Christ, you will be saved (Acts 16: 31). Being born again, being born anew, born from above or regenerated is a miraculous event, in that we dwell in the same old bodies, which has old habits and sinful tendencies, but we are renewed in our spirit. 2Corinthians 5: 17 says, "Therefore, if anyone is in Christ, the new creation has come: The old has gone, the new is here!" Since we have been made anew on the inside by the Spirit of God, we need to demonstrate this newness on the outside as people of God. The idea that regeneration comes to a person before he believes is quite interesting for some, even inspiring to others, but it is not biblical Christianity.

Questions to Contemplate/Discuss

    a. What is Regeneration?
    b. Who brings Regeneration?
    c. Who are regenerated?

d. How does Regeneration happen?
e. Why is Regeneration necessary?
f. In what way is Regeneration different from Justification?

CHAPTER 4

Total Depravity

4.1
What is Total Depravity?

We have so far shown much evidence in the Bible that Jesus Christ died for all men (2Corinthians 5:15), the world (John 3:16), and every man (Hebrews 2:9). Since Jesus has tasted death for every person, why are not all saved? Some persons reject Christ and refuse the gift of eternal life that is offered to them. Eternal life is given, but people must receive it by faith. However, some persons believe that the unsaved person is so wretched, worthless, and wicked that he cannot receive the gift of God that is offered to him freely.

Total Depravity is a reference to the state of mankind, after Adam and Eve sinned in the garden. Sin corrupted the person's entire being, which leaves him with a predisposition or propensity to sin. This tendency to sin causes some people to claim that the unsaved person must be given new life so that he can believe in Christ. The idea that a person needs to be regenerated before he can believe in Christ is found nowhere in the Bible. That is a philosophy that is not supported by Scripture. We want to take a careful look at what the Bible says on this issue of total depravity.

Some people define Total depravity as total inability. This definition is arrived at by interpreting the term "dead in trespasses and sins", as complete moral depravity. Physical death is the analogy used to present the case that a man cannot even believe in God. The lost man cannot receive a gift from God. The thinking, therefore, is that the unsaved person cannot even admit his sinfulness or his wretchedness because dead people cannot do any good thing. They should realize that a dead person can neither do good or bad.

You will soon discover that when you challenge that idea, the proponents of Total Depravity often will admit that an unsaved person can do good things. This they often reluctantly confess, because it does damage to their view of total inability. For example, it is clear to see, that the view that the unsaved person cannot do any good thing is false, because many unsaved people do countless good deeds. Unsaved people are sometimes more kind than some saved people. They don't oppress the poor or widow (Zechariah 7:10). They often give when they don't have much. They help the poor and widows, as we are commanded in scripture to do (Galatians 2:10). They support the orphans and take care of their community.

Unsaved people are known to have given their lives to save others whom they don't even know. They take care of their own children, which Jesus says they are able to do, and they provide for their spouses, and parents. Please note that I am not suggesting that these things make them justified or righteous before God. None of us is made righteous before God by our good deeds, but that does not mean that the deeds are not good. Jesus himself said in Matthew 7:11, "If you, then, though you are evil, know how to give good gifts to your children, how much more will your Father in heaven give good gifts to those who ask Him."

When some individuals talk about total depravity or total inability, they don't mean total in either case. Ask the individuals to clarify what they mean. What I am saying is, they believe that there is only one thing that the unsaved person cannot do, and that is to believe in Jesus Christ. They will admit that an unsaved person can believe in all other gods and do anything to please those gods, but they can't believe in Jesus. Isn't that a bit suspicious to you? Why can people believe in any other god but Christ? Their answer to that question is, because they must be regenerated first. This view is supported by their theological system, but it is contradictory to the Bible.

It is abundantly clear in Scripture that regeneration follows faith in God. I gave much evidence to this in the section that deals with regeneration. However, I think it is fitting to mention some of them here. Some people insist that in the same way a person could not contribute to his physical birth, the person also cannot contribute to his spiritual birth. We already agreed that no one can contribute by doing good works to earn his salvation or to be justified by his good deeds, because no good works will get us righteousness from God.

The brilliant thinker, John Lennox, noted in his book "Determined to Believe?" That verses like John 1:12, and John 5:40 show a "temporal priority that is simultaneously logical" (p. 191). So Lennox (2017) is saying that it is clearly obvious according to the order in Scripture that Faith precedes regeneration.

Ronnie Rogers in his brilliant exposition of John 3:14-15 makes the point that the text describes the exact sequence of how one receives life. Numbers 21:4-9 tells us how God delivered His people in the wilderness when they were dying because they were bitten by snakes. Rogers (2019) makes the point that it was after the people looked on the bronze serpent in obedience to God that they were given life. He explained that in the same way, only those who look to Christ for salvation will live (p, 67).

No one can contribute to being born again, but you must believe to receive it. That is just what the Lord has prescribed.

Norman Geisler, a very famous apologist for many years, insists that the Bible makes it plain that faith in God is logically prior to being regenerated or justified. Geisler (2001) argues that "there are no verses properly understood that teach regeneration is prior to faith. Instead, it is the uniform pattern of scripture to place faith logically prior to salvation as a condition for receiving it" (p. 237). This is so because faith is the means by which we receive the gracious gift of God's salvation.

The Apostle John tells us in John 20:31, that many miracles were done by Jesus, that were not recorded in the book, but these are written so that you may BELIEVE that Jesus is the Son of God, and that by believing you may have life in His name. Notice that BELIEVING comes before LIFE. Ephesians 1:12 tells us that when they believe the **Gospel of** salvation, they were sealed with the Holy Spirit until the day of redemption. Here again the sequence is faith in Christ and then life is given, or the Holy Spirit is given. Romans 1:16 says that the Gospel is the power of God unto salvation to everyone who BELIEVES. So again, we see that salvation or new life, eternal life is given to those who believe. John 1:12 says that God gave the right to some people to become children of God; those who put their faith in Christ, that is, those who receive Him. Abraham, David, Moses, and Elijah were all saved or made righteous, because they were justified by faith. This truth is clearly established in Romans 4:9-14 and Galatians 3:6-29.

All that is necessary for someone to believe is for them to hear the powerful life-giving Word of God that is able to penetrate bone and marrow; and the work of the Holy Spirit convicting them. We see in Scripture where God told people who were un-regenerated to choose life. This suggests that their depravity does not prevent them from choosing right and choosing God. The text even states that it is not difficult, nor is it out of their reach to trust God and live (Deuteronomy 30:10-20). God also made an appeal through His servant for unregenerated people to turn and live (Ezekiel 33:11).

This work of the Holy Spirit to the unsaved is to convict them of their sins so that they will see their need to repent (John 16:8-11). There is nothing that suggests that the Holy Spirit is doing anything else in those whom He convicts of sin, righteousness, and judgement. According to Romans 10:9-14, anyone, who hears the Gospel, is able to believe the Gospel and be saved. The same text tells us in verse 17, that faith comes by hearing the word of God. Therefore, all that is needed for the person to be saved is already provided. John the Apostle, in the Gospels stated that Jesus came and gave light to everyone. John declared this truth so that people would believe and be saved (John 1:7). Therefore, it means that people are able to believe when they hear the Gospel.

Some people teach a false doctrine that man must be regenerated or given new life before he can believe. They use the account in John 11 as their primary proof text to support their view. However, that passage of Scripture has nothing to do with conversion. The purpose of the text is to explain that Jesus is the Resurrection and the Life. If you believe the Scripture, you will not teach or even think that this text is describing how a person is converted. Remember that Jesus had recently been rejected in that town, and therefore the disciples did not want Jesus to return there. The disciples said to Jesus, "But Rabbi, a short while ago the Jews there tried to stone you, and yet you are going back?" (John 11:8). They were fearful of what might happen to Jesus and to them as well.

However, Jesus was set on going because He knew what He was going to do. He waited a couple of days until after Lazarus had died, so that He would accomplish this purpose. Jesus comforted the sisters and reassured them that they would see their brother again. This was not the resurrection they had in mind. They believed that Lazarus would be raised in the end times when all the righteous dead will be resurrected (John 11:24).

Jesus' appointment on this occasion was to prove that He has the power to give life, and that He is the source of life. Lazarus was already a believer in God and his family was anticipating meeting him again in the afterlife at the end. But Jesus caused them to meet him again in this lifetime by raising him from the dead. This is about resurrection, not conversion. A person can only see conversion in this text, if he carries that view to the text. That is clear eisegesis, where their own biases or presupposed ideas are read into the text.

Duvall and Hayes (2005) emphasize that the meaning of a text is the same for all Christians. Meaning is not subjective and does not change from reader to reader. Application, on the other hand, reflects the impact of the text on the reader's life (p. 179). It means, therefore, that we should not impose our meaning on the; rather, we need to take the whole context into consideration before we give any interpretation.

When Jesus said, "though he were dead," He meant, though the person was dead physically. That is the person that He raised physically. Even in this text Jesus said that He was doing this miracle so that the people might believe. Some of them did believe, while others refused to believe (John 11:45-46).

Grudem (1994) uses the term "total inability" to describe the moral and spiritual state of the unsaved person. He declares that, although the unsaved can do many good things in society he cannot do anything that pleases God (p. 497). This, however, is in contradiction to what we find in Scripture. For example, Cornelius in Acts 10:1-4 did what was pleasing to God, although he was not yet regenerated. I do agree, however, that no one can do enough good deeds to earn a place in heaven or to be made right with God through his own works. The Bible clearly teaches that Justification before God comes through faith; as we find in Romans 5:1-2.

When we examine the report of the conversion of Cornelius, we see quite clearly that the unsaved man along with his family was able to believe in Jesus, through the preaching of the Gospel and was regenerated. This is when the Bible says that Cornelius was given the Holy Spirit. The Apostle Peter said in Acts 10:47, "Surely no one can stand in the way of their being baptized with water. They have received the Holy Spirit just as we have."

This same unsaved or un-regenerated man Cornelius was a Centurion. He and his family were God-fearing and devout people. We are even told that God heard his prayers and that his prayers and gifts to the poor came up as a memorial before God (Acts 10:1-4). Again, let me make it plain; I am not saying that any of these good deeds earned his salvation. I am only saying what the Bible says, that this unsaved man was able to do good deeds and pray and seek after God, even though he was not yet regenerated.

The report in Acts 10:1-8 does not give the picture of a man who is totally depraved, in so much that he is unable to believe God, or trust Christ for salvation. In the book of Deuteronomy, we read in chapter 30:19, "This day I call the heavens and the earth as witnesses against you that I have set before you, life and death, blessing and curses. Now chose life, so that you and your children may live."

God was not playing games with the people by telling them to choose, because He knew full well that they are able to choose. Jesus told a group of Jews who refused to believe in Him, "Very truly I tell you, it is not Moses who has given you the bread from heaven, but it is my Father who gives the true bread from heaven. For the bread of God is the bread that comes down from heaven and gives life to the world" (John 6:32-33). So then, Jesus makes it clear that since the Bread of heaven was given to them, they only needed to receive it. The fact is that they rejected Jesus, not because they could not believe but because they would not believe.

Joshua in the Old Testament also confirms this fact that the un-regenerated person was able to choose whether to serve God, or to reject the true and living God and serve idols instead. He encouraged the people in Joshua 24:15 to choose whom they will serve. This truth is scattered throughout the Bible. A person would have to not want to see it, to miss it. For example, in 1 Kings 18:21-39, Elijah challenged the people to stop being 'wishy washy' in their faith. He said that it was time for them to choose whom they will serve. If it is proven that Baal is God, then serve him, but if it is evident that the Lord is God, then serve Him only. Elijah wanted the people to stop the syncretism. He was tired of watching them trying to mix their traditions with the tradition of other nations who worshipped idols.

We must allow the Scriptures to have final authority in our lives, and in how we believe. In Genesis chapter 3 we see where Adam and Eve ate the fruit that they were forbidden to eat and, they died as God had said they would. However, we also notice that they were able to hear God and speak with Him. They still knew what was good, and what was evil. Their off-springs, Abel and Cain, were also still capable of hearing God (Genesis 4:6-15), and doing that which pleases God (Genesis 4:4), and also of resisting or rejecting God. Please don't miss these insightful words! When Cain failed to please God, he was sad, and God said to him,

> Why are you angry? Why is your face downcast? If you do what is right, will you not be accepted? But if you do not do what is right, sin is crouching at your door; it desires to have you, but you must rule over it" (Genesis 11:4).

Cain could have, and should have done that which pleased God, but he did not. Notice that God made the point that Cain had the ability to choose right.

Sin always separates. The young man in Luke 15:11-31 was separated from his father, and Jesus describes that separation as dead. The young man was also lost because sin renders us lost and dead from the Garden of Eden, until now. When God asked Adam, "Where are you?" it was not to find out Adam's location but rather that Adam might realize his new condition.

I will now attempt to address some of the passages that are quoted in support of the erroneous doctrine. This doctrine says that man must be regenerated before he can believe and accept the gift of salvation. The book of Genesis mentions a period where the heart of man was said to be continually evil. In this very text in Genesis 6:5, the Scripture tells us that Noah found grace in the eyes of the Lord. Noah was a believer and a prophet of God. Noah and his family feared God. Therefore, the description that man's heart was only evil continually, though general, is not universal. The text in John 15:5, says a man can do nothing apart from God; Jesus was speaking about being fruitful and living a life that is pleasing to God. Anyone who reads the Bible can agree that apart from the help of God no one can live to please God. Verse 8 tells us that God's goal or purpose for us is that we will bear much fruit, because that is what glorifies Him.

Ephesians 4:17-19 is another proof text which is used to support their argument. However, all this text mentions is that believers must not live a meaningless lifestyle as those who do not know Jesus. It says that these people harden their hearts and have lost their sensitivity, so they give themselves over to sensuality. This is a similar description of those the Apostle Paul mentions in Romans 1:18-32.

These people suppressed the truth that was revealed to them. They wanted to produce their own righteousness and so they rejected the righteousness that God had provided. They became depraved and started worshipping created things rather than the Creator. God, therefore, gave them over to do what they wanted to do. Again, it is important to note, that in the context, it is describing those who suppress the truth by their wickedness (v,18).

In Romans we are told repeatedly that righteousness comes by faith (Romans 3:22), and that a man is justified by faith. Romans 1:17, says that the righteous live by faith. It is only by faith that one is given life, and it is by faith that one should live this life. We already agreed that no one can earn his salvation. We are convinced from Scripture that we cannot do enough good to be righteous before God. The Bible tells us in James 2:10, that if we break one command, we are guilty of breaking all of the commandments, because we become a law breaker. "All our righteousness is as filthy Rags" before a Holy God (Isaiah 64:6).

We need to note the context in which a statement is made to get the intended meaning of the author. For example, we often hear the quote of Romans 3:11-18 without looking at the text from which the Apostle Paul is quoting. He is quoting from Psalm 14:1-4, which says,

> The fool says in his heart, 'There is no God'. They are corrupt, their deeds are vile; there is no one who does good. The Lord looks down from heaven on all mankind to see if there are any who understand, any who seek God. All have turned away, all have become corrupt there is no one who does good, not even one. Do all these evildoers know nothing?

Remember that we already saw where Abraham, Joseph, Elijah, and others in the Old Testament walked by faith, and were listed in Hebrews as people who were made righteous by their faith in God. So, with that in mind we should understand that the author is not necessarily describing the heart and behavior of every single human being on the earth, but rather a description of all who refuse God; those who say that there is no God. Although all are sinners, not everyone lives a life that is described in Romans 3:11-18. Not everyone is swift to shed blood, although we are all law breakers. This truth is also found in Romans 1 which describes those who suppress the truth (v.18-32), in contrast to those who are just and therefore, live by faith (v.17).

1 Corinthians 2:14 says that the natural man does not understand the things of God, but he considers them to be

foolishness. He does not accept the things that come from the Spirit. In this text, the Apostle Paul is treating a situation where the people he is trying to reach are resting in human earthly wisdom. They are not benefiting from the deep truths of God because that must be revealed to a person by the Spirit of God. They refuse to submit to the wisdom of God. These believers who were living like the unsaved were not growing, nor were they able to understand the deep things of God. 1 Corinthians chapter 1 mentions the divisions in the Church, because the people were "carnal". In chapter 3 the Apostle Paul speaks to the fact that he could not give them the solid food of the Word of God, because they were not able to bear it.

Let us now look at John 6:44, which is a prominent proof text for those who teach that regeneration comes before faith in Christ. The verse says, "No one can come to me unless the Father who sent me draws them, and I will raise them up at the last day." The Apostle John explains that no one CAN come, unless he is drawn. But that does not mean that everyone who is drawn must come. Unless the persons who insist that they must come have some unknown method of how the Father draws, then we have to just stick with what is known in Scripture.

The text says that those who the Father draws, CAN come. That means that He enables them to come. So, whether they want to describe the word "draw" as to lead, to pull or to drag, it only makes people "able to come."

When a text poses a problem in understanding what the speaker is saying, it is helpful to look within the immediate or larger context to see if the speaker or author gives further commentary on the word or subject in question. This is crucial for proper exegesis, because a word has several ways in which it can be interpreted, because of its semantic range. For example, if I say the word "board" you would not know what I mean unless I put it in a particular context. Context is the key to understanding how a word should be understood and used.

Let me demonstrate. I could be using the word board to mean a piece of wood, or to get on a plane, or to lodge somewhere during college and receive meals and accommodation. I could be referring to the leaders or directors of an organization. Now, unless I give you the context, you can't know for sure what I mean. However, if I say that I nailed the board to the chair, you are able to tell how I am using the word board. Even if I said to you "I used the board to fix the chair and then I told the Board that we are now ready for the meeting, after which I must board a flight to Miami where I will board for college; although I used the word board in several different ways, you are still able to understand what I meant because of the context.

Let us now look back at the context in John 6. The ones Jesus promises to raise up are those that believe in Him (v 40). Those who eat His flesh and drink His blood are the ones who are given eternal life and are raised up (v 54). Jesus was not speaking of cannibalism here, because the people were not being asked to cut Jesus into pieces so they could eat His flesh. To come and eat of Him is to come and believe or trust in the supernatural Bread that is given by the Father to everyone. A person only needs to receive it. This is the Bread that came down from heaven which anyone may eat and not die (John 6:50).

Jesus explained how He was using the word "draw" in verse 44 by expounding or clarifying what He meant. Jesus says in v. 65, "This is why I told you that no one can come to me unless the Father has enabled them." So even if you do not agree with me about how the word was used, believe the Speaker Jesus, who tells us what He meant by the Father drawing. In the text, Jesus chose the term "enable" to explain what He meant, and His meaning has not changed.

Those theologians must stop insisting that drag is the word that communicates the true meaning of what Jesus was saying. They claim that the person is not dragged against his will. Therefore, they should stop using the example of someone pulling a net of fish because it does not truly express their claim, because the fish is not made willing. But they claim that the person is first made willing before he is dragged to Christ, on their worldview. There is a conflict in their doctrine, because they hold tightly to the picture of something being pulled against its will, and then constantly apply it to someone who they claim is not being pulled against his will.

The woman at the well in John chapter 4, came because she was able to come to Jesus. There is nothing in the text that suggests that this sinner was given anything other than the life-giving word of God as Jesus spoke with her. Her heart was evidently convicted, which is what the Holy Spirit is here to do in the life of sinners today, and she trusted in Jesus the Messiah. Jesus told her to ask, and she will receive living water (John 4:10). Jesus also tells us in Matthew 7:7, "Ask and it will be given to you; seek and you will find; knock and the door will be opened to you." This invitation is not only for Christians, but for all who will seek God. Acts 17:26 says, "From one man He made all nations, that they should inhabit the boundaries of their lands. God did it so that they would seek Him, and perhaps reach out for Him and find Him, though He is not far from any one of us."

There it is, clearly stated in Scripture; this is how God has designed it all. He created mankind but after the fall, God first sought us out in the garden, and also by sending Jesus Christ to die on the cross for our sins. Jesus says to us in John 12:32, "And I, when I am lifted up from the earth, will draw all people to myself." He said this to indicate the kind of death He was going to endure; the death on the cross. Jesus is still drawing people through the cross today. Remember, to draw does not mean regenerate.

Questions to Contemplate/Discuss

a. What is Total Depravity?
b. Are Human beings totally depraved?
c. Is the un-regenerated blind, deaf, and dead like a corpse?
d. Is one regenerated before one believes?
e. Can the unregenerated hear and believe the Gospel?

CHAPTER 5

Irresistible Grace

5.1
What is Irresistible Grace?

The term Irresistible Grace is a teaching that whoever God wants to save, will be saved, because God has already regenerated their heart so that they will want God. So, the person will not resist God, because God has revived his heart, and his desires are changed.

The God of heaven, "… gives everyone life and breath and everything else" (Acts 17:25), also gives mankind the freedom to make choices. This does not mean that man is able to do whatsoever he wants, because it is a freedom that has boundaries. God allows human beings to choose to serve Him or to reject Him. However, man is not allowed to choose the implication or the consequences of those choices. The consequences are decided by the Law Giver, not the law breaker.

Remember, we already witnessed the evidence of Scripture that shows that regeneration always follow faith in God. We see nowhere in the Bible where regeneration precedes faith. All we need to do now is to look at the evidence of Scripture which shows that people can, and do resist God's grace and salvation. Jesus said to the people who were rejecting Him, that the Father has given them the True Bread from heaven (John 6:32). However, they refused the Bread. John 5:40 also states "Yet you refuse to come to me to have life." According to Jesus, the reason they did not have life is because THEY refused to come to Him.

The Apostle Paul tells us why the people perish. He says in 2 Thessalonians 2:10, "They perish because they refuse to love the truth and so be saved." Acts 7:51-52 says, "You stiff-necked people! Your hearts and ears are still uncircumcised. You are just like your ancestors; you always resist the Holy Spirit! Was there a prophet that your ancestors did not persecute?" These persons, who were seeking to stone Stephen, were rejecting the Word that is able to save their souls. They got angry, and stoned him to death. The Book of John makes it plain in chapter 3:19 when it says, "This is the verdict: Light has come into the world, but people loved darkness instead of light because their deeds were evil." This is the Son that came and shined into the world and provided light for everyone. They resisted the light as we saw in John 1:7-11.

In the Old Testament God was angry with His people, because He did so many wonderful miraculous things for them, yet they refused to trust in Him. Hebrews 3:19 tells us that some of the Israelites did not enter God's rest because they did not believe. In the following chapter the Author makes the same point, warning his readers to not miss out on entering the rest of God like the people in the Old Testament did (Hebrews 4:6).

Here is something that is very important to note; God is not trying to save people, and failing to do so. His plan was to save only those who believe. Therefore, those who refused to believe are not the people God is saving. Would we say that God is trying and failing with Christians who are not growing consistently in their faith and obedience? No, we would not! It is God, who sets it up this way, to save people who believe in Him (1 Corinthians 1:21).

Questions to Contemplate/ Discuss

a. Can a person resist the Holy Spirit?
b. How can a person resist the Holy Spirit?
c. What is the evidence in Scripture that people resist salvation?

CHAPTER 6

Sanctification

6.1
The Concept of Sanctification

Sanctification is one of the terms in the Bible that is often used in a Preacher's sermon; but it is also often misused in its application.

Let us examine what Scripture says about sanctification, and then see if we can apply the concept appropriately. The word "Sanctify" means to set apart or to make holy. In the Bible, when used to speak regarding inanimate things or objects, it means to be consecrated or set aside for service to God. When it is used regarding salvation, it means to make holy or to separate for holy purposes. That is, set apart as holy for the service of God.

6.2
The Contents of Sanctification

When we read the Bible, we get a good glimpse of what sanctification entails. The Scriptures present sanctification in three phases or distinct periods and stages of change and development. The Bible speaks of sanctification which affects or impacts our past status before God. Before we were sanctified, we were not seen as, or called, saints of God. Now that we are in Christ, we are called saints. Please note that this is referring to our position in Christ. The believers at Corinth were called saints in Christ, not because they were living a godly lifestyle, but because they were considered holy by God, through the righteousness of Christ that was put on their account, when they trusted Jesus Christ for salvation.

Our positional sanctification speaks to the fact that God has separated us from the penalty of sin, and we are now regarded as His own. The Apostle Paul wrote in Romans 8:1, "Therefore, there is now no condemnation for those who are in Christ Jesus." Jesus also says in John 5:24, "Very truly I tell you, whoever hears my word and believes Him who sent me has eternal life and will not be judged but has crossed over from death to life." We also read in John 3:18, "Whoever believes in Him is not condemned, but whoever does not believe stands condemned already because they have not believed in the name of God's One and only Son."

Sanctification begins at regeneration, but it does not stop at conversion. God wants to deliver us from the power of sin in our day-to-day experiences. Our past sanctification impacts our position before God, but our present sanctification impacts our practice before God and man. Now that we are made saints in our standing, we are to be saintly in our living. This does not mean that we are perfect or sinless, but it means that we are committed to ordering our steps to work in God's Will. No one does what is right all the time and never sins (Ecclesiastes 7: 20).

6.3
The Command to Sanctification

We are commanded in the Word of God to sanctify ourselves by putting aside the sins and habits that will defile us. The Apostle Peter tells us in 1Peter 2:1-2, "Therefore, rid yourselves of all malice and all the deceit, hypocrisy, envy, and slander of every kind. Like newborn babies, crave pure spiritual milk, so that by it you may grow up in your salvation." Since we have received of the Lord's goodness, we ought to feed on His Word that we might grow. This is the spiritual food that will help us to mature in our faith and obedience to God.1Corinthians 6 tells us that some of the believers in the church used to live wretched and immoral lives. The Author listed some of their past habits as sexual immorality, idolatry, theft, adultery and drunkenness. However, in verse 11 he says, "And that is what some of you were. But you were washed, you were sanctified, you were justified, in the name of the Lord Jesus Christ and by the Spirit of our God." The Apostle Paul is saying, they are not the same people that they used to be.

One of the things that will help us to be good and godly examples for Christ is in knowing who we are; and whose we are. The Apostle Paul often reminds the believers about the fact that they are saints in Christ, and a new creature in Him (2 Corinthians 5:17). The Bible also lets us know that it cost God a lot to purchase our salvation (Hebrews 10:8- 14). Our salvation comes to us free, but it is not cheap, because we have been bought with the precious blood of Christ in whom we believed (Hebrews 9:11-14). We are also told in 1 Corinthians that we were bought with a price, and we must therefore glorify God with our bodies (1Corinthians 6:20). This same fact is repeated in 1 Corinthians 7:23.

The Psalmist asks a question in Psalms 119:9 where it says "How can a young person stay on the path of purity? By living according to your word." The Psalmist has made a commitment to live a life of purity, and he tells us how he was going to accomplish it. He says "I seek you with all my heart; Do not let me stray from your commands. I have hidden your word in my heart that it might not sin against you" (Psalm 119:10-11). Therefore, if we abide in God's word and His words abide in us, we will be able to live a sanctified lifestyle.

In spite of the challenges we face as saints in Christ, we are still able to resist the temptation and please God (1Corinthians 10:13). Philippians 2:12 instructs us to work out our salvation with fear and trembling. Note that the Apostle did not say that we should work "<u>for</u> "our salvation, but rather that we must work it "<u>out</u>." He was not suggesting that the believers should work to attain or to maintain salvation. What he was addressing was the fact that the saints must live out their new identity. He wanted them to live out what they believe; not only in his presence but even more in his absence. This is an important point because sometimes Christians seek to do right depending on who is seeing them. He is saying, wherever we are, God is, and He is the one we should be living to please, instead of pleasing men (Gal. 1:10).

The Apostle Paul is telling the believers why they are able to live right. Verse 13 of Philippians 2 says "For it is God who works in you to will and act in order to fulfill his good purpose." By ourselves we are not able to walk in obedience to God's will, but if we rely on the help of the power of the Holy Spirit and humble ourselves, we will be victorious. James 4: 7 says, "Submit yourselves, then, to God. Resist the devil, and he will flee from you." We will not be victorious over the devil when he tempts us if we do not first summit ourselves to God. For God opposes the proud, but gives grace to the humble (James 4: 6).

Although we will not live a perfect and consistently holy lifestyle in this body, the Bible tells us what to do to be pleasing to God. Roman 6: 11 says that "In the same way, count yourselves dead to sin but alive to God in Christ Jesus." Now being dead to sin does not mean that we are not able to sin. It simply means that we are to consider ourselves separated from sin, having no relationship with it. If we refuse to count ourselves as being cut off from sin; as having no relationship or intimacy with sin, we will lose the battle that is going on in us.

Presently, there is a war going on inside the members of our bodies. The Holy Spirit wants to be in control so that we will be led by Him. Galatians 5:16 states, "So I say, walk in the spirit, and you will not gratify the desires of the flesh." This does not mean that we will no longer have bad desires; it only means that those bad desires will not have us. We will not be controlled by the desires of the flesh, but by the leading of the Holy Spirit. Therefore, we are encouraged by the Apostle Paul to not quench the Holy Spirit (1Thessalonians 5:19), and to not grieve the Holy Spirit (Ephesians 4:30). If we set our minds on heavenly things (Colossians 3:1), and if we seek the Lord with all our heart, we will be pleasing to Him. 1 Thessalonians 4:3 says, "It is God's will that you should be sanctified: that you should avoid sexual immorality." Believers are not only set apart <u>from</u> something they are also set apart <u>for</u> something; which is to glorify God.

6.4
The Comfort of Sanctification

Purity pays! It is to our benefit that we live pure. Proverbs 24:3 says, "Above all else, guard your heart, for everything you do flows from it." Jesus also tells us that out of the abundance of the heart a person speaks (Matthew 12: 34). We will be rewarded for a life of faithfulness. The difficulties, hardships and struggles that we face in this life as we strive to live pure, are not worthy to be compared with what we will receive (Romans 8: 18-19). There is also coming a day when we will be perfectly sanctified. By that I mean, the manifestation of the completion of our sanctification. This is when we will be delivered from the very presence of sin. Our mortal bodies will put on immortally (1 Corinthians 15: 42), and we will be like Jesus. For John says, "We are now the Sons of God, but it has not yet been revealed what we shall be, but we know that when He appears we shall be like Him, for we shall see Him as He is (1John 3:1-3). Be encouraged by this truth.

Questions to Contemplate/Discuss

a. What is Sanctification?
b. What is the process of Sanctification?
c. Who are sanctified?
d. What does it mean to be saints in Christ?
e. When will our Sanctification be completed?
f. What are the different phases of Sanctification?
g. How can we live a sanctified life?
h. What are the benefits of living a sanctified life?

CHAPTER 7
Redemption

7.1
What is Redemption?

Redemption is one of the great themes of the Bible from Genesis to Revelation. There are several parts that make up the whole of redemption. We want to consider some of the key issues in redemption.

The first thing we want to mention is why there was a need for redemption in the first place. The word redemption means to purchase. It was often used of the situation where someone was paying for the freedom of someone else. The need for redemption arose because mankind had sinned by disobeying God's commands in the Garden of Eden (Genesis 3:6). This failure carried it with it several consequences. For example, the promise of death was fulfilled right there at the very moment that Adam and Eve sinned. God had warned them that in the day they eat of the fruit that he commanded them not to eat, they shall surely die. This act of disobedience caused both Adam and Eve's death that day. This was a spiritual separation from God. They were separated from the life of God, although they were still alive physically (Genesis 3:8-9).

The second implication was that Adam and Eve no longer had the desire to be intimate with God. When they heard God coming in the garden they ran and hid themselves, because they were afraid and ashamed. While they were hiding, God was seeking them out. God called out to the man saying, "Where are you?" (Genesis 3: 9). Even unto this very day mankind is still hiding and running away from the Holy God of heaven, because mankind is still afraid and ashamed to be in the presence of a Holy and Righteous God.

Not only did Adam's sin affect or impact human beings who would come after him, but it put the human race on enemy line, because they were born with a bent or predisposition toward sin. It is like the head of your clan or family being at war with the king, and it puts the rest of the family in a position where they too are cut off from all the blessings and privileges of being with the king in his kingdom. Adam and Eve were cast out of the garden, because God did not want them to eat of the Tree of Life and live forever in that state of sin.

We want to make a distinction between just existing and receiving eternal life from God. God said that Adam and Eve would live forever if they were to eat the fruit of the Tree of Life (verse 22). However, this is not the life eternal that God offers. Even people who are not trusting God for salvation will exist forever; but only those who believe in Him will have eternal life. This is not about the quantity or duration of life, but it's about the quality of life; the very life of God (John 3: 16).

When mankind fell, all of creation was impacted; so that even the earth and the animals groan for the redemption of the sons of God (Romans 8: 22). The following verse states that we ourselves groan inwardly waiting for God's full redemption. This is when all will be made new, both believers and the whole creation. Those who refuse to trust in Christ will miss that glorious day. The impact of man's disobedience left him dead in trespasses and sin. He is no longer intimate with God. Human beings have a predisposition toward sinful tendencies which cause them to be slaves to sin. Humans also lack righteousness and holiness to stand in the presence of God.

7.2
The Practice of Redemption

It was because of Mankind's fallen status that there was a need for redemption. Let us look at the practice of redemption. Deuteronomy 24:18 says, "Remember that you were slaves in Egypt and the Lord your God redeemed you from there." God was reminding His people that He is the Redeemer. When they were in bondage in Egypt, God saw their troubles; He felt their pain, and He delivered them from the hand of the Egyptians and Pharaoh. In our recent history, we see the cruelty done to slaves by those who held them captive. People were buying slaves, but not for the purpose of freeing them. The slaves only had different owners, who kept them in bondage of the worst kind.

7.3
The Person of Redemption

Since mankind was in a very bad situation, being dead in sin and separated from God, they needed someone to pay for their redemption. No other human being could have accomplished this task, because the wages of sin is death (Romans 6:23) Therefore, if anyone were to die **for** his/her own sin, he/she would be dying <u>in</u> his/her own sin, which would make the payment without value to God. That sacrifice could not satisfy the requirement of the Holy God.

God loves the world, so He does not want to punish people. However, God is also a Just and Holy God; so, He must judge sin and punish the sinner. God did not just forgive the sin of mankind, but He sent His Son to pay for our sins. Jesus was the only person qualified to pay the price of sin, for He alone is worthy. He alone is Holy. He alone is perfect and without blemish or sin.

7.4
The Price of Redemption

The price for redemption came at a very high cost. Jesus did not send an angel to pay; He came as the convener of the offering, and to be the offering. Hebrews 9:22 tells us that without the shedding of blood there is no forgiveness. Therefore, Jesus had to die and shed His blood in order for redemption to be realized. The writer of Hebrews says, "It is impossible for the blood of bulls and goats to take away sins" (Hebrews 10: 4). God did not want people to offer animals' blood for their sins anymore, so He sent the "Lamb of God" who takes away the sin of the world (John 1:29). Those offerings of animal's blood served only as a covering for mankind's sin. It was just a shadow of the greatest and final sacrifice that was to come. Hebrews 9:12 says of Jesus, "He did not enter by means of the blood of goats and calves; but he entered the most Holy Place once for all by his own blood, thus obtaining eternal redemption."

7.5
The Purchase of Redemption

Sometimes a person might desire to buy something, but the price is too high and so they just walk away. The price of redemption was really high; it cost God the Father, the blood of Jesus His Only Begotten Son. However, He thought it was worth it. It cost Jesus Christ so much pain, shame, rejection, and the burden that comes with bearing the cross, but He thought it was worth it. We are told in Matthew 20:28, "Just as the son of man did not come to be served but to serve, and to give his life as a ransom for many."

Even Jesus' disciples did not understand why He had to die to accomplish Redemption. One day two believers were walking on the road to Emmaus, when Jesus joined the conversation. They spoke about how the Chief Priests and rulers handed Jesus over to be sentenced to death. When Jesus was crucified, they did not understand. They were confused, because, according to their understanding, the Christ was not supposed to die, but to come and redeem the Nation of Israel. They knew of a redemption, but they were not aware that it was purchased by the blood of Christ (Luke 24: 20). Hebrews 9:15 says, "For this reason Christ is the Mediator of a new Covenant, that those who are called may receive the promised eternal inheritance now that he has died as a ransom to set them free from the sins committed under the first covenant."

When Jesus died on a cross at Calvary, He paid the full price for man's redemption. Just before He died, He cried "It is finished." This means that the debt was paid (John 19:3). The Bible tells us in Galatians 4:4, "When the set time had fully come,

God sent His Son, born of a woman, born under the law, to redeem those under law, that we might receive adoption of sonship." I will speak to the concept of sonship later.

7.6
The Period of Redemption

Please note that Christ was slain on the cross at Calvary in time; not before time began. He was not slain before the foundation of the world as some versions of the Bible translate it. The text actually says that Christ was slain **from** not before the foundation of the world. The word "**appo**" which means since, or from, is used in the Greek text. If the writer wanted to say before, he would have used the word "**pro**" which means before. Many scholars know this fact, but they still repeat the error of translating the word "**appo**" as "before," because it supports a doctrine that they wish to keep. Revelations 13:8, states that the Lamb was slain after sin entered the human race. The Apostle Paul tells us that when God saw it fit, He sent His Son. This same Jesus gave His life on Calvary once and for all. 1 Peter 1:20 says, "He was chosen before the creation of the world but was revealed in these last times for your sake." Please note that although Jesus was chosen (elect) from before time began, He came and died for the sins of the world when the time was right according to God's plan.

7.7
The Product of Redemption

In the 5th chapter of the book of Revelation, we are introduced to a worship scene where we hear the worshippers saying, "You are worthy to take the scroll and open its seals, because you were slain, and with your blood you purchased for God, persons from every tribe and language and people and nation" (Revelation 5: 9).

So, what did the atonement produce? What is the result of Jesus dying on the cross and being raised from the dead? Be careful to note before we go any further, that Christ's death by itself did not redeem anyone. If Jesus Christ did not rise from the dead, then everyone would still be in their sins. 1 Corinthians 15: 12-19, makes it very clear that if Christ did not rise from the dead, the Apostles would be telling lies that He did. This would mean that no one is really saved, and your faith is futile, and life is meaningless. Therefore, as we speak about the atonement, bear in mind that the resurrection is the seal of Christ's sacrifice. This is why The Apostle Paul tells us in Romans 4:25, that Jesus was raised for our justification. This was the evidence that the payment was accepted.

We also learn that God was appeased by the sacrifice of Christ. Isaiah 53:6 says, "We all, like sheep have gone astray; each of us has turned to our own way; and the Lord laid on him the iniquity of us all." Here we see that God gave His Son to bear the sin of the people, so that He would not have to destroy the people. Therefore, God is able to be just in punishing sin, but still be the justifier of all sinners who trust in Christ for salvation (Romans 3: 26). Verses 10 -11 of Isaiah 53 informs us that the

Father was pleased to crush Jesus. This is a description of what Jesus endured. Yet, the text also said that the Father was satisfied. He was pleased with what was accomplished. He enjoyed the fruit or the produce of the atonement.

7.8
The Planet was Redeemed

The extent of Jesus' redemption is for the whole planet. I am not suggesting that Jesus' sacrifice caused every man, woman, boy, and girl to be saved. I reject that idea, because the Scripture does not support that teaching. What I am saying is that Jesus' atonement was made for all. No one is excluded.

David Allen, who is arguably the most prominent Scholar on the subject of the atonement, says "here we have God himself offering salvation to all, but how can He do this according to limited atonement, since there is no provision for the Salvation of the non-elect in the death of Christ. Furthermore, how can God make this offer with integrity?" (p. 786) Here again Allen makes a case from the Bible for the universal extent of the atonement using primarily for the core texts 1 Timothy 2:1-6 and 2 Corinthians 5:11-21 among many other Bible verses.

When we look at the atonement that was practiced in the Old Testament, we understand that the atonement was made for all Israel, but then only those who drew near would benefit, as seen in 2 Chronicles 29:24-25. The Writer of Hebrews says that Christ has tasted death for every man (Hebrews 2:9). Over and over the claim from Scripture is that Jesus 'atonement was for the whole world. There is no other way for God to say it through His Apostles and Prophets to make it any clearer in His Word. A man would have to close his eyes to not see this plain truth in Scripture. Some have seen it, but they do not want to say it because it contradicts their doctrine.

Not only does the Bible tell us so many times, but it tells us in many different ways. For example, Hebrews 2:9 says, "But we do see Jesus, who was made lower than the angels for a little while, now crowned with glory and honor because he suffered death, so that by the grace of God He might taste death for everyone." It is clearly stated that Jesus has tasted death for everyone. We find also in Titus 2:11, "For the grace of God has appeared that offers salvation to all people." 1 Timothy 2:3 says, "This is good, and pleases God our Saviour, who wants all people to be saved and come to a knowledge of the truth. For there is one God and one mediator between God and mankind, the man Christ Jesus, who gave Himself as a ransom for all people."

If we are willing to allow the Bible to have the final say about whom Jesus Christ died for, then it is clear that He died for the whole world. The well-known and well-loved words of John 3:16 tell us that God loves the world. The following verse says that God did not send His Son into the world to condemn the world, but to save the world through Him. The Apostle John uses the word "cosmos" to refer to the inhabited world, or the people who live on the earth, or the created universe. John 1:10 tell us that the world was made by Him. We see in some text that Jesus came to give light to the world, which is referring to the people. The Apostle John also instructs us in 1 John, that we must not be drawn to the world system that is in constant hostile rebellion against God. John says that we must not love the world, nor the things of the world (1 John 2:15.17). He is not telling us not to love people, but rather that we must not love the system which is driven by lust and pride. If we seek to love that world system, we will not love God, who is opposed to that system.

It is clear that these passages are not referring to Christ dying just for the elect, but for the whole world. This world, the Apostle John states, does not know us (1 John 3:1). John tells us why the world does not know us, and it is because the world did not know Jesus. Again, he speaks of the world under the power of the evil one in 1 John 5:19. This is referring to the devil having this world under his control. We have no reason to deny the truth about the devil's influence, because we can see the manifestation of it even in our communities and in our countries (although I must let you know that this is allowed by the Sovereign God).

Notice how the Apostle John uses the word, world; it is in reference to the whole inhabitants of the earth, or that rebellious system that rejects God and the people of God. John 15:18 says that the world hates the believer, because it first hated Christ.

Here in john 14:16-17 Jesus sought to encourage His disciples because they were sad and broken hearted because He told them that He will soon be leaving them. Jesus said, "If you love me, keep my commandments and I will ask the Father and He will give you another advocate to help you and be with you forever, the Spirit of truth. The world cannot accept Him because it neither sees Him or knows Him. But you know Him, for He lives with you and will be in you." The Apostle John also warns about false prophets that have gone out into the world (1 John 4:1). He informs us of the victory that believers have in Christ, that makes them overcome the world (Revelation 12:11), so we are conquerors though Christ.

As we can clearly see, none of these verses is referring to a specific group of people who are elected for salvation. To insist that Christ died only for a specific group of people, and then restrict or change the clear meaning of the word "world", as it is used by the author, is plain arrogance or ignorance, both of which can cause someone to mishandle and misrepresent the Scripture. We can believe the Scripture when it says that God loves the world and gave His only beloved Son, so that whoever believes in Him will not perish but have everlasting life (John 3:16).

Jesus is the Lamb of God who takes away the sins of the world (John 1:29). Jesus is also said to be the sin offering for the whole world. John tells us that this offering was made for everyone. Note what he says in 1 John 2:1-2, "My dear children, I write this to you, so that you will not sin. But if anybody does sin, we have an advocate with the Father, Jesus Christ the Righteous One. He is the atoning sacrifice for our sins, and not only our sins but also for the sins of the whole world." Can it be any clearer than this? What else does Scripture need to say to convey the plain truth that Jesus died for the whole world? Scripture uses different words and different phases so that we would not miss this truth. The Scriptures say that Jesus died for all men (2 Corinthians 5:15), for every man (Hebrews 2:9), and for the world. If Scripture is our final authority, our hearts should then be bowed to this truth; that Jesus' death was an offering for everyone.

Some persons try to escape the powerful grip of this truth, by committing the negative inference fallacy. This is where a person seeks to use inclusive statements, as exclusive statements. For example, they will point to Scriptures that state that Jesus died for the sheep (John 10:11), for His Sheep (Acts 20:28) and that He laid down His life for the sheep (John 10:15). It is easy for me to admit that Jesus Christ died for the Church, but I also know that the people who make up the Church, are also a part of the number that make up the human race for which Jesus died.

Therefore, pointing to those verses or any other in the Scriptures will not be sufficient to derail the consistent and clear passages that say Jesus Christ died for the whole world. If I report to you that I was speaking with a man at the Post Office yesterday, who told me all that I needed to get my letters, and then later you hear me giving the same report about the post office experience, but now I mention that I spoke to two men, who advised me what to do to get my letters, would you accuse me of lying about the number of persons I spoke with at the post office? Unless I had stated in the first report that I spoke with ONLY one person, you cannot accuse me of lying. I chose only to mention one person when I spoke to you, because of the purpose of that conversation; that does not mean that I am lying, because I told others about the other man who helped me.

So, the fact that some persons show verses that state that Jesus died for the sheep, His sheep or the Church, does not mean that His death was only for them. Those who try to use this tactic to escape the truth about the extent of the Atonement of Christ, prove to be inconsistent when they are interpreting Scripture. For them "all" only means all, in places where it does no damage to their theological system. World is changed to mean elect where it suits their purpose.

It is the context that should determine for us how a word is to be interpreted. The context is the key to giving the meaning to the text. Notice when Scripture says that all have sinned, that "all" means all, but when Christ died for everyone, for the world and for all, that changed to the elect. Why then is it not said that Christ died only for the Apostle Paul? Paul said in Galatians 2:20, "I have been crucified with Christ and I no longer live, but Christ lives in me. The life I now live in the body, I live by faith in the Son of God, who loved me, and gave himself for me." Notice how many times in that verse he used the words I and Me. Are we to believe that Christ died only for Paul? Therefore, it is clear how erroneous their type of hermeneutics would become if it were done consistently. That is why they are very inconsistent in their approach as they deal with the atonement of Christ, and for whom the sacrifice was made.

7.9
The Plan of Redemption

How then are we to understand the impact of the atonement? Please do not miss this truth. Jesus' atonement was made for all, but only benefits those who believe. While Jesus was on the cross, one thief was at His right and another thief on His left. The crowd was also there watching Jesus dying on the cross. Many of these people cried, "crucify Him." Some may have spat upon Him and mocked Him. Even the thief at the right hand, who later confessed Jesus and trusted Him for salvation was railing at Jesus earlier, before he came to his senses and saw that Jesus was truly the Saviour (Matthew 27:44).

Although the offering was made for all, God's plan was not to save all for whom Jesus died, but rather, to save all those who trusted Christ for salvation. Luke 19:10 says, "For the Son of Man came to seek and to save the lost." However, not all lost people are saved, because not all lost people trust in Jesus for salvation. In Romans 5:8 the Apostle Paul tells us, "But God demonstrated His own love for us in this, while we were still sinners Christ died for us." This is the second time that the Apostle Paul states this same truth in just two verses apart. He earlier states in verse 6 that when the time was right, when we were still powerless, Christ died for the ungodly. Again, we see that Christ died for all sinners, and only sinners who trust in Christ will be saved.

The Apostle John states that Christ came to His own; which is referring to His own people Israel. They, however, rejected Him, but all those who received Him, to them He gave the power to become the children of God (John 1:11-12). These people are given life from above when they believe in Christ. John 3:16, tells us that those who believe in Christ will have eternal life. The Apostle Paul tells us in Romans 6:23 that eternal life is a gift.

Now, here is where we cannot miss this plain truth of Scripture and logic. This gift only benefits those who RECEIVE it. This is what we see in Scripture. The word, "receive" in John 1:12 is an active verb which implies that the receiver or beneficiary must accept the gift. Notice in the text that some rejected Christ, which means that they rejected life. And some received Christ, which means that they accepted the life, which makes them children of God. God is not less kind because some people reject the gift of eternal life.

It was always God's intention to save those who believe. We are told repeatedly in Scripture that those who believe are made righteous (Romans 3:22), are justified (Romans 5:1), and are saved (Ephesians 2:8). Jesus paid the price even for false prophets who are damned because they denied the Lord. 2 Peter 2:11 says, "But there were also false prophets among the people, just as there will be false teachers among you. They will secretly introduce destructive heresies, even denying the Sovereign Lord who brought them, bringing swift destruction on themselves." Notice that it is this same Sovereign Lord who paid the great price and bought the saints. The same word that is used for bought in 2

Peter 2:1 is also used for bought in 1 Corinthians 6:20, where it says that the Church is bought with a price. The gift must be received to get its benefit. We are told in 2 Peter 3:9 that it is not God's Will that any should perish but that all should come to repentance. I will expound on this verse later.

The persons who continue to try and make John 10:15 about sheep verses goats are being misled or are trying to mislead. The text is not speaking about whether God gave Christ to die for sheep and not goats. The passage is speaking about the Jews who were rejecting Jesus. Jesus was saying that they are not "His sheep." The ones who listen to the Father, listens to the Son also (John 6:45). Those are the sheep that belong to the Father, whom the Father also gives to the Son. There were people who believe in God, who did not yet know about Christ. These people understood and obeyed the words of Moses.

They identified the words of Moses as the Word of God to them. Now Jesus makes the point that if they had believed Moses, they should have believed Him. But since they do not believe Moses, they are, likewise, rejecting Him (John 5:46). Let me say this truth another way. Jesus was saying: the fact that the Jews were rejecting Him is proof that they did not believe Moses. This point is clear in Scripture because sheep follow their shepherd (John10:27-30).

Something else is crucial to note here, there were some faithful followers of God, who listened to the voice of God, and therefore will also listen to the Son as well. All the Jews who were true followers of God came to accept the Son as well because they acknowledged Him as the Messiah. The Son speaks the same way as the Father and, therefore, He could be identified as the promised Savior. They could identify the Messiah by the message He brought.

None of the passages in John that speaks to salvation speaks about sheep versus goat. Please don't confuse Matthew 25:3, because this is referring to the Lord judging the nations in the end. In the Book of John, the goat is not a sinner and the sheep a saint. All sinners are sheep, but they are not Christ's sheep. And all the saints are sheep who are now Christ's sheep. The topic of the text in John, is whether one is a follower of God. The point Jesus is making is that sheep listen and follow their shepherd. Therefore, Jesus was saying to them that they are not His sheep because they do not listen and follow Him, nor His Father, nor Moses (John 5:31-46).

I wish to address one more issue in this section. The Bible makes it clear that faith is the prerequisite to receive eternal life (John 3:16, 18). It amazes me whenever I hear persons trying to make faith out to be a work that one does to "save himself." Faith is contrasted with the works of the Law repeatedly in Scripture. For example, Romans 4:13-15 says,

> It was not through the law that Abraham and his offspring received the promise that he would be heir of the world, but through the righteousness that comes by faith. For if those who depend on the law are 'heirs, faith means nothing, and the promise is worthless.

The Apostle Paul explains through the rest of the passage that salvation is by faith, and not by the works of the Law. So, Abraham was given righteousness because of his faith in God and not because of the works he has done (Romans 4:3, 11, 22).

In Romans 4:23 it says that God did not mention the word "credited" for Abraham's sake alone, but it was written for our sakes as well, who God "credits" with righteousness when we believe. The Apostle Paul makes it abundantly clear as he said in Romans 3:28, "For we maintain that a person is justified by faith apart from the works of the law." The gift of salvation is not applied like the trespasses (Romans 6:15). This is true because the gift must be received by faith in Jesus.

Jesus is the bridge to God, and the only way a person can be saved is to step on that bridge by faith. Now, please don't take this analogy beyond what it is meant to convey. We already saw in Scripture where it clearly states that faith in God is not working for your salvation or "saving yourself." The person must believe that Jesus is the only way or path to the Father, and unless he connects with God through faith, he will not enter God's grace according to Romans 5:2. The Apostle Paul says, "Therefore, since we have been justified through faith, we have peace with God through our Lord Jesus Christ" (Romans 5:1). It is through faith in Christ that we gain access into this grace in which we now stand (Romans 5:2). Therefore, salvation was purchased for everyone, but it is only applied to those who believe. This is so because eternal life is a gift which must be received to benefit the person.

Questions to Contemplate/ Discuss

a. What is Redemption?
b. What is Atonement?
c. Why did Jesus have to die to pay for our sins?
d. When was the price paid for sin?
e. What does Propitiation mean?
f. Why was it necessary for God to be appeased?

CHAPTER 8

Reconciliation

8.1
What is Reconciliation?

Now that we have a clearer understanding of the state of mankind after the fall, and the fact that God has sought out human beings to offer them His great salvation; we can move on to study how reconciliation works.

Remember we said earlier that "All have sinned and come short of the glory of God" (Romans 3:23). We also said that the "Wages of sin is death" (Romans 6:23). An important point to make here is that God seems to make provision for all those who die before they are able to respond to salvation. For example, infants who die before they reach a state of maturity; whereby they would understand how to choose the good and reject the bad. Isaiah 7:15-16 tells us of a time when the child does not yet know how to choose the good, and refuse evil. Notice also, that when David's child died after he was born, David said the child will not come to him, but he will go to meet the child (2 Samuel 12:23). This shows that David understood that God makes provision for persons who are not able to choose to accept God's offer of salvation to them. This would also be true of persons who are born with a state of mind that is not able to understand because of mental problems from birth.

Some persons reject this idea because they hold to a philosophy which states that only those whom God has picked from before the foundation of the world will be saved. God has made provision through reconciliation for all people. Therefore, we can agree that no one is reconciled to God because they have saved parents. God's work of reconciliation was done for the whole world, but it must be received by the individual. I cannot accept Christ for my children, nor can they do it for me.

We will now look at a definition for the term Reconciliation. Reconciliation in the Bible refers to God choosing to repair and restore harmony in a relationship that was broken because of mankind's sin. After mankind sinned against God, there was hostility between us and God, because mankind has developed a predisposition towards sin, which causes him to run from God, and push against God's Will. Mankind on a whole rejected God's means of salvation and restoration, and has tried to establish righteousness on his own terms.

8.2
The Reason for Reconciliation

There is a beautiful passage of Scripture in 2 Corinthians 5:11-21, which gives us some insight about how reconciliation works. Notice that the text tells us that Christ died for all, which means that all were dead. But those who live; that is, those who have eternal life, "should no longer live for themselves but for Him who died for them and was raised again" (v15). Therefore, there is a distinction being made in the text between those for whom Christ died (all) and those who now live (have life). The latter are the ones who have life, and they must not live for themselves, because they have been bought with a price (1 Corinthians 6:20, 7:23, 1 Peter 1:19). The intention of Jesus Christ is to reconcile people through His shed blood. (Colossians 1:18-20). This could only be accomplished by Christ because we cannot rescue ourselves. So, God sought to restore fellowship with us through His Son.

8.3
The Reach of Reconciliation

According to Colossians 1:18-21, the price that Jesus paid on the cross served to reconcile the whole world; including the earth. The same truth is also stated in 2 Corinthians 5:19, "That God was reconciling the world to himself in Christ, not counting people's sins against them. And has committed to us the ministry of reconciliation." So, the deliverance for the whole world was purchased and this is why the creation is groaning for the final redemption of the people of God because at that time creation itself will be made new (Romans 8:19-20). The reconciliation of Christ is far reaching. Matthew 13:44, gives us a picture that the whole world is paid for.

8.4
The Response to Reconciliation.

God has made provision and reconciliation for the whole world through the cross of Christ, but it is only applied to those who receive it. Jesus tells us in John 12:32, that when He is lifted up (crucified), He will draw all men unto Himself. After Jesus was raised from the dead for our justification (Romans 4:25), He offered salvation to whoever will receive it. Two thieves were on the cross beside Jesus, one received salvation by accepting Jesus Christ as his Lord, while the other perished in his sin for rejecting Jesus; although Christ died for both of them.

Jesus likened the crucifixion on the cross to the bronze serpent that was lifted on a pole by Moses in the wilderness. We mentioned it earlier, but it is appropriate to mention it here as well. The people of Israel were dying, because they were being stung by snakes. God had caused this to happen because of their disobedience and unbelief. God commanded Moses to make a bronze serpent and lift it on a pole so that whoever is stung by a snake would not have to die. They only needed to look on the bronze serpent on the pole and live (Numbers 21:4-8). Jesus likened Himself to that situation when we read John 3:14-15, "Just as Moses lifted up the snake in the wilderness, so the Son of Man must be lifted up, that everyone who believes may have eternal life in Him."

Please don't miss that key point here. Notice who will have eternal life; those who believe. So, although the offer of the gift of eternal life is to everyone, it is only given to anyone who believes. This means that each person has a responsibility to respond to God's offer. Verse 21 of 2 Corinthians 5 says that people must be reconciled to God. Please note that the text tells us that God has reconciled the world unto Himself (v18), but people have a responsibility to respond by being reconciled to God (v20). This is accomplished by trusting in Jesus for salvation. If your answer to God's offer is "no", your reply will determine where you spend eternity. God has made an abundant provision of grace (Romans 5:17), and therefore the Apostle Paul says God commands all people everywhere to repent (Acts 17:30).

8.5
The Result of Reconciliation

What reconciliation through the cross accomplished is harmony between God and man, when we receive His gift of eternal life. Ephesians 2:14-16 tells us that Christ has brought Jews and

Gentiles together as one in Christ and has broken down the dividing wall between them; therefore bringing peace. He has reconciled both to God. The result or effect of reconciliation on believers, should be evidenced by our fruit-bearing. The Apostle Paul tells us in 2 Corinthians 5:17 that, "If anyone is in Christ, the new creation has come." He also makes the point in verse 15, that we should no longer live for ourselves; but for Christ who died for us and rose again. The reality is that we are not our own, we belong to God because we have been bought with a price (1 Corinthians 6:20).

Let us examine this text a little more closely. We are, according to the writer, Ambassadors of Christ. An ambassador is one who represents a king or a country or an organization in an official capacity to deliver or speak on their behalf. The Apostle Paul is saying that we are God's officials, sent by Him to represent Him to others in the world. Please note that the ambassadors are sent to represent the will, words, and desires of the king; not their own.

The ambassadors are sent to serve the king and his kingdom agenda. Hence, the agenda of God for His servants is that they make an appeal. Notice verse 20 again it is, "As though God were making His appeal through us." Isn't that wonderful that the God of heaven would include us as workers together with Himself in the process of reconciling the unbelieving world? Hallelujah! Therefore, we need to be about the Master's business. We need to get up and get going. Time is running out. We have wasted enough opportunity to reach the lost. What matters to our King should matter to us because we are His Ambassadors. People's soul matter to our King; it should also matter to us as well.

Questions to Contemplate/Discuss

a. What is Reconciliation?
b. Who does the reconciling?
c. How did God reconcile the world to Himself?
d. What did Reconciliation accomplish?
e. What are Ambassadors of Christ sent to do?
f. When last have you shared the Gospel with someone?

CHAPTER 9
Predestination

9.1
What is Predestination?

There has been much debates and contention over the topic of Predestination, than any other subject in the Bible. That is primarily because much of the debate is not based on what the Scriptures say, but rather it's based on the view of a well-loved Pastor or Teacher or Theological System. I would like to contribute to the discussion on the topic of Predestination, as well. Please note that my treatment of this topic is intended to do a study on the word Predestination, where it is referring directly to people who are saved.

There are things that are ordained by God which we can speak about in another chapter, but for now, let us focus on the four verses that deal with the believer's salvation. I will be using the inductive method to investigate these passages, and pull from the text what is said, what it meant, and how it applies to us today.

Let us begin with a definition of the word Predestination. The word Predestination really means to appoint beforehand. It is to decide or arrange the destination prior to the journey. For example, as a coach I might promise the players in the community that all those who come with me on the bus will receive a medal when we reach Negril. I have decided beforehand what is going to happen to those persons who come on the bus. I have also decided or ordained that before they even set foot on the bus. I did not, however, put anyone on the bus. Yet, what will happen to them at the end of the journey has been decided by me. Furthermore, it is only those who accept my invitation and join me that will benefit from what has been pre (before) destined.

It is important to note, that it is not everyone who is on the field who will receive the medals that I promised, but only those who are in the bus at the point of destination, Negril. In the Bible, the spiritual gifts and blessings are in Christ. The phrase "in Christ" is significant to the believers' inheritance. Here are a few references that speak to our status and blessings in Christ. 2 Corinthians 5:17, says if anyone is "in Christ" he is a new creation. We have been made alive "in Christ" (1 Corinthians 15:22). 1 Corinthians 1:2, says that we are sanctified "in Christ." We are called wise and righteous "in Christ" (1 Corinthians 1:3). 1 Corinthians 15:22 says that "in Christ" all shall be made alive.

According to the Apostle Paul in Galatians 3:26, we are children of God by faith "in Christ." Believers are partakers of the promise "in Christ" (Ephesians 3:6). He calls believers the "Faithful in Christ" (Ephesians 1:1). In verse 3 of the same chapter, he says that believers receive all spiritual blessings in heavenly places "in Christ." We are seated in heavenly places "in Christ" (Ephesians 2:6). We are God's handiwork created "in Christ", to do good works (Ephesians 2:10). We have been brought into intimate relationship with God, because we are "in Christ", we are no longer enemies (Ephesians 2:13). I took the time to show these verses without any exposition, because these are verses that make it plain, that it is because of the entity that we are in (Christ) that we have all the status and spiritual blessings.

Persons who hold to Exhaustive Divine Determinism, which is the idea that God has ordained from before the foundation of the world all things that come to pass. This teaching posits that God has predestined some unto conversion and others, unto damnation. That is their view of what predestination is about.

However, predestination in the Bible is about blessing and inheritance, in Christ. Now let's look at the biblical evidence for this. In Ephesians 1:5 we read "He predestined us for adoption to son-ship through Jesus Christ, in accordance with His pleasure and will." Note that it is God who predestines. Note also, who are predestined; believers. We see in the first verse that it is speaking about saints or the faithful in Christ. So, it is those who are in Christ that are predestined. What are they predestined to? "Unto the adoption of sons." That means the adoption that belong to sons, or that sons get.

Adoption in this context is not like adoption in our 21st Century adoption in the Western World. The adoption here is speaking about a child receiving his full inheritance having come to an age of maturity. It's about what the child gets. This is a saint receiving the inheritance when the fullness of time comes. It is not about God predestinating a sinner to conversion, but rather, its saints to glorification. Adoption is not how one gets into the family of God. It is about how one must be born again through faith in Christ, and therefore receive the Spirit of adoption.

The believers' full adoption is still future; and we as Christians all wait for it at the end. Until then we have been given the Spirit of adoption which serves to mark us for Christ, showing that we belong to Him. Galatians 4:4-6 says, "But when the set time had fully come, God sent His Son, born of a woman, born under the Law, to redeem those under the Law, that we might receive adoption to son-ship." The context explains from verse 1-3, that the heir is already a son, but he is not ready to receive his full inheritance of sonship.

Romans 8:15, says that believers have received the Spirit of Adoption, which enables them to know that they belong to God (verse 16). In his efforts to encourage the believers in Rome who were going through immense persecution and many of them dying, the Apostle Paul told them it will get better in the end. He told them that their suffering cannot even be compared with what they will receive (verse 18). He made it clear that our adoption is the redemption of the body (Romans 8:23). This is what all of creation awaits and groans for. As believers we long for the day of redemption, when we will be given our new bodies (v 23).

The Apostle John tells us in 1 John 3:1-2,

> See what great love the Father has lavished on us, that we should be called children of God! And that is what we are! The reason the world does not know us is that it did not know him. Dear friends, now we are children of God, and what we will be has not yet been made known. But we know that when Christ appears, we shall be like him, for we shall see him as he is.

Therefore, although we are children of God now, we are not experiencing the fullness of our adoption, which is the redemption of the body, to which we have been predestined (Ephesians 1:5).

The Apostle Paul tells us that we have been "Predestined according to the plan of Him who works out everything in conformity with the purpose of his will" (Ephesians 1:11). There is nothing in this verse that even suggests that God predestined unbelievers to conversion before the world was. The text is explaining that God is presently working all things to accomplish His purpose and will. Note that this working of God is in the present tense and not something that was done before creation.

Where else in the Apostle Paul's writing do we read about God working things to accomplish His purpose? Romans 8:28, informs us that God works all things together for good for them that love God and are called according to His purpose. The clear reading of the text does not fit the narrative of determinism. Determinists claim that this verse demonstrates God's work in salvation from eternity past. However, this verse is pointing to what God is doing presently in the life of believers in Christ. It is specified to the faithful in Christ or those who love God. So, this is not referring to everyone, but to those who love God.

In Romans 8:29, the Apostle Paul says, "For those God foreknew he also predestined to be conformed to the image of His Son." Romans 8:28-30 tells us that the people who are predestined are those who love God. They are saints in Christ. The text tells us that they are predestined, not to conversion, but to "be conformed to the image of His Son." This is referring to our full adoption, redemption, and glorification; when we will be like Jesus (1 John 3:1-2). None of these verses speak about anyone being predestined to conversion or of sinners being predestined to salvation before the world was created.

We see a lot of people today who are turned off from God and the Bible because they have heard what Theistic Determinists say about predestination, but that is not what Scripture says. The negative effect of that teaching from the Determinist's perspective has also caused some Christians to claim that they don't believe in predestination. This is also wrong, because predestination is taught in Scripture and so we should believe the Bible and not the Determinist's view on the doctrine.

Let me share one last point from the text in Romans 8. The passage could be referring to believers in the Old Testament who trusted God through persecution and God worked all things together for good for them because they loved Him and were called for His purpose. This is possible because the Apostle Paul spoke about the Old Testament saints who trusted God. This is also a reasonable option because he used the past tense, when he mentioned that those God foreknew He predestined, and those He predestined to be conformed to the image of His son, them He also called.

There are two "Calls" in Scripture; a Gospel call (Romans 10:9-14, 2 Thessalonians 2:14), and a Vocational call (Ephesians 4:1, 2 Corinthians 5:20). Those who are called are justified, and those who are justified are glorified. In light of the fact that glorification of the New Testament believers is set for the future, and the glorification in this text is in the past tense, it could be referring to believers in Old Testament. They are being used by the Apostle Paul to show us an example for how God will deliver and work things out for good for believers today, just like He did in the past. I think the text could also be referring to believers today, and he is using the past tense because our glorified bodies are already predestined. We will one day be changed when our mortal bodies have put on immortality (1 Corinthians 15:50-58, 2Corinthians 1:21-22).

The word "foreknew", in the text could be referring to those who God knew before in a relational way. That is, those with whom He has a relationship. God is omniscient; therefore, He knows all things and all people, but not in a relational or intimate way. For example, Jesus says that in the end many will come saying, "Lord, Lord, did we not prophesy in your name and in your name drive out demons and, in your name, perform many miracles? Then I will tell them plainly, I never knew you. away from me, you evil doers" (Matthew 7:21-23).

As we examine this text, we recognize that Jesus is aware of who they are because He knows them, but not in an intimate way. With this truth before us, we can be sure that He knows those who belong to Him (2 Timothy 2:19). Furthermore, the Apostle Paul told some believers in Galatians 4:8-9, that there was a time when God did not know them. This was when they were unsaved. God did not know them. Even in the Old Testament the term "know" was used to express intimacy.

Predestination means that the destination, which is our glorification or being conformed to the image of Christ, is already determined by God from before the world was. Just as my analogy suggests, God does not pick anyone from before the foundation of the world, to go on the bus, but He has predetermined what will happen to those who are on the bus. Christ was the chosen One, even before mankind was created. When we got into Christ, we also became the chosen of God. In Christ, we will reach the destination which goes beyond conversion, but to inheritance and glorification. (Ephesians 1:5, Romans 8:23, Ephesians 1:11-14, Romans 8:29, and 1 John 3:1-2).

Questions to Contemplate/Discuss

a. What is Predestination?
b. Who are Predested?
c. To what are they Predestined?
d. What is Adoption in the Bible?

CHAPTER 10

Election

10.1
What is the Meaning of Election?

We have now come to another of the doctrine of the Bible, which engenders the most controversy and debate. In Romans 9, the Apostle Paul speaks about what God is doing with His people and accomplishing His purpose. If one does not follow the argument closely, and carefully, one might come away from the text believing in Exhaustive Divine Determinism. This philosophy claims that God has decreed or ordained everything that happens in the universe. This decree, it is believed, includes everything that happens, both good and bad. Those who hold to the philosophy of divine determinism, also claim that God has picked some people to be saved and others He left for damnation, from before the world was created. Romans chapter 9 is the core passage for this philosophy. However, if we keep reading to the end of the Apostle Paul's argument in Romans 11, we will realize that he is speaking about something completely different from determinism. Let us go through the text and see what we find.

The Apostle Paul starts at the beginning of chapter 9:1-3 to speak about his great sorrow and anguish of heart over the people of Israel because they were rejecting Jesus. At this time of his writing, the Israelites were rejecting their Messiah, and therefore, not fulfilling their purpose as witnesses for God. They were supposed to be a light to other nations, but they were not. They were chosen to be God's mouthpiece to the nations of the world. God's choice of Abraham was not to condemn the rest of the world, but to be a blessing to the rest of the world. All the other families of the world were blessed because of Abraham, because he was chosen for that purpose (Genesis 12:3). When we understand election, in the context of God choosing Abraham and his family out of all the families of the world, we will realize that this election is about missions. This is a picture of God reaching the world through a particular group of people.

The word Election simply means to choose. It is about something, or someone being chosen for a particular blessing or task; as seen in the promise given to Abraham (Genesis 12:3). God had promised Abraham about his descendants' role in preparing the way for the Messiah, and spreading the message to other nations. It was through Abraham's descendants that God would bring the oracles. The believers could not understand why the Jews were constantly resisting and rejecting the Gospel of Jesus Christ.

The Christians in Rome were somewhat bothered or concerned that the Apostle Paul continued to go to the Jews and to the Synagogue, where he is being rejected and sometimes persecuted. They only saw his effort as a waste of time, and a cause for further persecution. He, however, had a different view on the matter. The Roman believers thought that God's promises had failed.

The Apostle Paul explains that God's promises had not failed, because some Israelites were still being saved through the Gospel and were fulfilling the missionary work to which they were called. He uses himself as evidence that God's purpose is still being fulfilled, seeing that he is an Israelite who is spreading the Gospel. Romans 9:4-5, points to the fact of the privileged position that Israel has being given. There are many blessings and honor that come with being the people that God has chosen. For example, the Apostle Paul mentions their adoption, divine glory, covenants, laws, temple worship, and promises as unique privileges to them because of the Patriarchs from whom the Messiah would come.

He again makes it clear in verse 6 that God's promise has not failed, because not every Israelite is being referred to as "Israel." The Israel that God is going to use to bring forth His mission and message of salvation are those who trust in Him. Therefore, not all Israelite will have a role in bringing about the missionary function for which God has chosen Israel.

10.2
God's Choice of the Boys

Let us pay close attention to who was chosen in these verses, and for what they were chosen. The Apostle Paul says in Romans 9:10-12, that Rebekah was told by God that she was going to have twins and the children in her womb will represent two nations (Genesis 25:23). God has chosen Jacob to be the son through whom He will bring the line of the Messiah and the message. God said that the older would serve the younger. This is significant, because normally in that culture, the younger would be responsible to serve the older. God was turning around the practice of the culture for His own purpose and glory.

Something we need to note in this text, is that Esau was chosen to "serve" Jacob. It does not say that Esau was chosen before he was born to be condemned to hell. That idea is read into the text and is therefore, eisegesis. It is used by those who want to teach a theological system that does not come from the Bible. Remember that Esau and Jacob represented two nations (Genesis 25:23). Jacob, the younger brother (Israel), should be served by Esau, the older brother (Edom). The nation of Edom did not serve Israel, but rather persecuted them. Therefore, God hated Esau (Edom), because Edom did not make life easy or better for his younger brother Israel (Malachi 1:2-3). This is what the Apostle Paul is speaking about in Romans 9:13. When God said, "Jacob have I loved and Esau have I hated," the boys themselves were already dead and gone over a hundred years before.

God was speaking about the older brother Esau (Edom), the nation that made life bitter for the people of Israel. When God gave the promise to Abraham He said, "I will bless those who bless you, and whoever curses you I will curse; and all the peoples on the earth will be blessed through you" (Genesis 12:3). God fought against Esau (Edom) because Edom was fighting against Jacob (Israel). God had cursed Edom because Edom did not bless Israel. In Deuteronomy 23:7, God warned the Israelites to make sure that they treat the Edomites with kindness, because they are brothers (Jacob and Esau). However, Edom was not kind to Israel in return, and God promised to take revenge (Ezekiel 25:12-14). Geisler (2001), also holds to the same view that I am positing here, that the reference to Jacob in Romans 9:11-13, which says, "Jacob have I loved, but Esau have I hated," is not the man Jacob, but the nation Israel and its reference to Esau, is not to the man Esau, but to the nation of Edom (p. 84).

The Apostle Paul also mentions the choice of Isaac over Ishmael. This does not mean that Isaac was chosen for heaven, and Ishmael was chosen for hell. God's election (choice) of Isaac was to bring the line through which God will bring the Messiah into the world. Abraham had Ishmael before Isaac, and he had other children after Isaac. Does that mean that Ishmael and the children born to Abraham after, went to hell since they were not "Chosen"? Anyone claiming that those who were not chosen were damned to hell, did not get it from the Bible, but from somewhere else!

The Apostle Paul asked a question in verse 14 of Romans 10, that needs to be understood in the context of the discussion. So far, He has explained that God's promises had not failed. Israelites are still being saved, and God's election of the twins was about their service, and not about their salvation. He had just reminded us that God chose Isaac over Ishmael, and Jacob over Esau which is contrary to the way people are chosen in that culture. Therefore, we hear him asking "Is God unjust" (verse 14)? To which he responded, "Not at all."

The Apostle Paul then quotes Exodus 33:19, where God says, "I will have mercy on whom I will have mercy, and I will have compassion on whom I will have compassion." This text says nothing about heaven or hell. The context was saying that God chosen not to destroy His rebellious people that day. However, I do not think anyone would want to claim that all those who were spared by God's mercy that day received eternal life. Mercy is a gift that God gives to persons who deserve to be punished. God had the right to destroy them, but He chose not to. It is the act of God, whereby He withholds the penalty that our behavior deserves. This verse also does not tell us who God wants to show mercy. However, we are later plainly told that God wants to show mercy to all (Romans 11:32).

God's choice of Abraham, Isaac, Jacob, and the nation of Israel was not about salvation, but for service. They were blessed to be a blessing to all nations of the earth (Genesis 12:3). Therefore, God's election in the life of those people was not based on their goodness or badness, but only that God's plan of election might stand.

10.3
God's Choice of Pharaoh

God's choice of Pharaoh was to glorify Himself throughout the world. Please do not lose the Apostle Paul's train of thought here. Let us look back at the context of Egypt and the people of God. The people of God were in Egyptian bondage, and they were being treated badly (Exodus 3:7). The Lord saw what was happening to His people and sought to intervene. Moses was chosen by God as the one who would lead them out of bondage. God knows the heart of all human beings, and so He told Moses that Pharaoh will not let the people go. God knew that Pharaoh was wicked and stubborn and, therefore, He chose to use him. Pharaoh was oppressing the people of God, and God wanted to rescue them and bring them out of that land. Exodus 3:7 says, "The Lord said, 'I have indeed seen the misery of my people in Egypt. I have heard them crying out because of their slave drivers, and I am concerned about their suffering."

The land of Egypt was filled with the practice of idolatry, which the Lord hates (Exodus 20:3). God wanted to use this opportunity to prove to the world that He alone is God, and there is no other that deserves worship. Isaiah 43:10-12 says, "You are my witnesses, declares the Lord, and my only servants whom I have chosen, so that you may know and believe me and understand that I am He. Before me no God was formed, nor will there be one after me. I, even I, am the Lord, and apart from me there is no Saviour. I have revealed and saved and proclaimed. I, and not some foreign god among you. You are my witnesses, declares the Lord, that I am God." Isaiah also tells us in chapter 44:6, "This is what the Lord says Israel's King and Redeemer, the

Lord almighty: I am the first and the last; apart from me there is no God."

God, by His awesome power used several plagues to prove that the gods that the Egyptians worshipped were powerless to save. God used these events to demonstrate that there is no other God but Him, which was the conclusion of the story of God's deliverance of His people in Egypt. God did not destroy the Egyptians all at once, but He used the situation to cause a wicked Pharaoh to become more stubborn and fixed in his attitude of rebellion against Him, which is the hardening that Scripture is speaking about.

Please note that God was not hardening a godly man in the person of Pharaoh, but God was really using a wicked rebellious man, whom He knew would not surrender to His Will. Although it is true that God uses even wicked people to accomplish His purposes, as we will see later. He is not the One who makes them wicked. In Scripture there are numerous occasions where God used the wickedness of man to show the goodness of God. Let us look at some of these passages.

We just saw how God used Pharaoh to accomplish His purpose, and to show His power and goodness. Now we will look at how God did the same through Joseph's brothers. Genesis 37:1-11, gives us a picture of what was happening in Jacob's home. It was a home filled with contention and jealousy; problems from the parent right down to the children. We will only focus our attention on the jealousy and hatred that the brothers had against Joseph.

Genesis 37:2, tells us that Joseph informed on his brothers, and it was not a good report. The following verse tells us that Jacob loved Joseph more than any of his other sons. God had gifted Joseph, and had given him dreams, and the special ability to interpret dreams. Joseph's brothers already hated him because he was the father's favorite and he would report their bad behavior to their father when they misbehaved. However, it got worse when Joseph told them about the dreams God gave him. The text says that they hated him even more and could not speak to him kindly (Genesis 37:14). They then sought opportunity to destroy him.

One day as Joseph went out into the field to meet his brothers, they decided among themselves to kill him. However, Reuben tried to rescue him by telling the rest of the brothers to throw Joseph into a pit. This Reuben did because he planned to come back for Joseph and bring him home to his father. While Reuben was away from the other brothers, some merchants passed by, and the brothers sold Joseph to the merchants who took Joseph to Egypt where he was then sold as slave to a man called Potiphar (Genesis 37:12-28, 39:1).

It is important to note at this juncture, that Joseph's brothers were jealous, proud and wicked, according to the Scripture. God knew that they were wicked and bad minded, so He used their evil hearts to accomplish His good desire. God knew that a famine was coming, and He used the brothers' hatred of Joseph to get Joseph into Egypt, where he became Prime Minister and was able to save his people. As Joseph later reflected, on the circumstances of his life, he was able to say to his brothers in Genesis 50:20, "You intended to harm me, but God intended it for good to accomplish what is now being done, the saving of many lives."

It is, therefore, clear if we are following the text, that God did not make Joseph's brothers evil or cause them to hate Joseph and to do evil to him. God in His providence, however, used what they intended for evil and turned it for good for the people, and brought glory to Himself; which was His intention all along. The fact that God uses someone who does evil does not mean that God makes that person do the evil. God is redeeming the situation of evil; not causing the evil in the situation.

There is a story in Isaiah 10:5-19, where God used a wicked king to discipline His people, because they had turned their backs on Him and were worshiping false gods. After God had used the wicked king as His instrument to discipline the Israelites, He judged the wicked king for his sins and for taking the glory for being victorious over Israel. Again, God did not make the king wicked, but He wanted someone who would be willing to do it and the king was the one. Repeatedly in the Bible, we see where God used wicked persons to accomplish His purpose in the earth. When God wanted to punish His children for their sins, He would often use wicked people as His instrument to do it. This does not make the people who are being used to accomplish God's purpose innocent, because God is only using them in their wickedness and not making them wicked.

Here are some passages that support that point (Judges 3:7-15, 4:1-3, 6:1-10). And this is the same thing we see in Daniel 4:28-37, God gave king Nebuchadnezzar great power, but he became proud, and God judged him for it. Nebuchadnezzar started to take glory for himself. He said, "Is not this the great Babylon I have built as the royal residence, by my mighty power and for the glory of my majesty?" God brought him low, and he repented, confessed, and praised the God of heaven (Daniel 4:34).

Let us now look at one final example of how God used the wickedness of individuals to accomplish His purpose. I want to first remind you, that we should take care to rightly divide the

Word of God, by examining the context and noting what is said in the passage. If we refuse to do that, we will either attribute things to God that He did not do, or attribute things to someone else that God did.

In the crucifixion of Christ there are many parts that make up the whole. We want to examine the text to see who played what part, and how they contributed to the whole event. Firstly, Mankind had sinned and was separated from God. Mankind could not rescue itself, so God sent His Son to be the Saviour of the world. This was not going to be a universal salvation where everyone is saved, but a universal offer that anyone who believes will be saved (John 3:14-18). God has set it up where the one who will be made righteous must believe, which is to trust in God. Now, please note that I am not saying that faith is what saves us; it is God who saves those who put faith in Him. God is the Saviour and the object of our faith.

Jesus came and died for the sins of the world, whereby He tasted death for everyone (Hebrews 2:9). Christ did this because man could not pay for his own sin and be made right with God. Therefore, Jesus gave His life as a sacrifice for sin (Hebrews 9:11-12). Hebrews 9:22 says, "Without the shedding of blood there is no forgiveness." The author says, "It is impossible for the blood of bulls and goats to take away sins" (Hebrews 10:4).

Who are the persons who played a role in the crucifixion? What role did they play? Are they culpable of evil? God had ordained that His Son will be the Redeemer of the world (Isaiah 53:1-13). So, He sent forth His Son to accomplish salvation. Mankind could not be forgiven without Christ's blood being shed (Hebrews 9:22). Therefore, God used some people who hated Jesus, and those who had other agenda to profit themselves from the situation.

For example, Judas wanted to profit from the capture of Jesus, because he was a thief and a lover of money, and not of God (John 12:6, Matthew 26:15). So, Judas sold Jesus for thirty (30) pieces of silver. It was already prophesied that Judas would do this. The Chief Priest, elders and the high priest also played a role in plotting to kill Jesus, and to bring false accusations against Him (Matthew 26:1-5). Pilate played a role when he chose friendship with Caesar over friendship with the Saviour. Pilate himself knew that the Jewish leaders wanted to kill Jesus because they were jealous of Him (Matthew 27:18). Pilate even called Jesus a just man, and that he found no fault in Him (John 18:38, 19:6). When the Jewish leaders realized that Pilate wanted to release Jesus, they said that if he released Jesus, he is not a friend of Caesar (John 19:12). Pilate chose King Caesar, and the applause of the Jewish leaders, rather than Jesus, and the applause of God.

Yet, although so many people played a role in the event, God's purpose of redemption was still being fulfilled by allowing wicked men to kill Jesus; which is the way He chose to accomplish salvation. Therefore, when we read Acts 2:23 that, "This man was handed over to you by God's deliberate plan and fore knowledge; and you, with the help of wicked men, put Him to death by nailing Him to the cross," it was God in His providence, working things for good and His glory. God's role in this event was orchestrating the process, so that the plan of salvation that He foreordained would come to pass, even through the freely chosen acts of wicked men.

So, we have seen where the Father played a role. Pilate and the leaders of the Jews played a role, and the people who were bribed and motivated to crucify Jesus played a role. Jesus also played a role because when He was being questioned by Pilate,

Pilate told Him that he had the power to set Him free. However, Jesus told Pilate, that he only had power in the situation because it was given to him from God (John 19:11). Jesus in John 10:18 says, "The reason the Father loves me is that I lay down my life, only to take it up again. No one takes it from me, but I lay it down of my own accord." Acts 4:27-28 says, "Indeed Herod and Pontius Pilate met together with the Gentiles, and the people of Israel in this city to conspire against your holy servant Jesus whom you anointed. They did what your power and will had decided beforehand should happen." What is God's role here? He decided or decreed before, that the death of Christ would happen and that it would be by crucifixion (John 3:14, 12:32-33).

To make sense of these passages, we need to note carefully who is doing what. God was not sinning or doing something evil when He gave His Only Begotten Son (John 3:16), nor was He being wicked when He crushed Jesus on the cross for our sins (Isaiah 53:10). Jesus laid down His life; it was not taken from Him. So, although Judas sold Jesus out for thirty (30) pieces of silver; Jesus was already sold out to the Father's will. Remember, Jesus Himself said that He could have called His Father, and His Father could have sent angels to fight for Him (Matthew 26:53). Nevertheless, Jesus said in Luke 22:42, "Not my will but thine be done."

What we have seen in the passages we have looked at, is how God is able to use persons in their rebellion and wickedness to still accomplish His purpose in the end, like we see in Pharaoh and the deliverance of God's people. We also saw in Joseph's life, how God in His providence, turned things around and protected Joseph. Joseph went from being thrown into a pit, to being sold to Potiphar in Egypt, to be falsely accused and be cast into prison, and in the end to be promoted as Prime Minister in the Palace.

I took the time to go through those verses to give some clarity to the often misunderstood verses in Romans 9:17-18. We will now return to the flow of the Apostle Paul's argument in Romans 9:19, where he is presenting what an objector would say, based on the reason he gave, as to what God is doing with the Jews. Just like Pharaoh, the Jews at this time were rebelling against God; and God was hardening them, just like he did Pharaoh, and the people who hated and crucified Jesus.

Now, listen carefully to this objector. Paul said that God was being glorified and accomplishing His purpose through their rebellion. That is true, because it is the rejection of Jesus as Messiah, which led to the Jews killing Him. It is the resistance to the Gospel which caused it to be taken to the Gentiles who were being saved by faith in Jesus Christ (Romans 9:30-33; 11:11). The objector is saying, "Since our evil is bringing glory to God and His will is being accomplished, why does God still blame us?"

The first thing the objector got wrong, is that he believes that God should be pleased with him even if he does evil; as long as God gets glory from it (Psalm 50:21). However, my sin stands on its own before God, regardless of what glory God brings to Himself. Their rejection and rebellion were bad, but the Gospel going to the Gentiles was good. Now, the good that God accomplished through their evil does not make their evil praiseworthy.

The second thing that the objector got wrong, is that he thinks that no one can resist God's will. This view is clearly false, because the Jews in general were resisting God's will. Luke 7:30, tells us that the Pharisees and experts in the law rejected God's purpose for them. Many persons resisted and rejected God's will for their life, as we will later see in the Scripture. The Apostle Paul was showing several examples of people who rejected God's purpose for them and rebelled against His will. When persons resist God's purpose for them, He uses them for another purpose to glorify Himself. This was true of Joseph's brothers, Pharaoh, the leaders who plotted against Jesus, and the Jews who were rejecting the Apostles and the Gospel of Jesus Christ.

If we follow the Apostle's argument, it is easy to identify the objector. The objector, for all logical reasons, is a Jew who is being told that he is rejecting the Gospel and the Messiah, but God is still being glorified because the Gentiles are being saved. The Jew is hearing the Apostle say that God is using Israel for a different purpose, because they have rejected the Gospel and salvation by grace through faith. So, the Jew doesn't think it is fair for God to judge him for his rebellion, and also now use him for a different purpose, if God is still getting glory through his disobedience. The Jews in general were rejecting the Gospel, and the Gentiles were now hearing and receiving it. This objector does not think that it is fair; because they are God's chosen people.

The objector despised the idea that Israel's God would harden His own nation and show mercy to those who were not called His people. This is what Hosea prophesied. Romans 9:25-26 says, "I will call them my people who are not my people; and I will call her my loved one who is not my loved one, and, in the very place where it was said to them, you are not my people, there they will be called children of the living God." It is important to note that God can show mercy to whom He wants to show mercy. This does not mean that all the Gentiles who heard the Gospel were being saved, only those who trusted in Christ.

The Apostle Paul then responded to the anticipated Jewish objector by telling him that the Potter has the right to do with the clay what pleases Him. Therefore, the objector is out of order to argue with the Potter. Immediately, his readers who know the Word of God would understand the analogy about the Potter and clay in Jeremiah 18. God wanted to tell Jeremiah something about what He was going to do with His people Israel, so He gave him an object lesson. God sent Jeremiah down to the Potter's house, and there he saw a Potter working on the wheel. However, the pot he was shaping from the clay was marred in his hands. So, the Potter formed it into another pot, shaping it as seemed best to Him. Then the Lord asked Jeremiah, "Can I not do with you, Israel, as this potter does?" (Jeremiah 18:1-12).

The point that the Apostle Paul makes is that the vessel (Israel) was marred or spoiled. God did not spoil the vessel. The vessel became hard and resistant to the working of the Potter. Israel was not pliable in the hands of the Potter. Therefore, since the Potter's purpose is being resisted, and the Potter has other purposes to accomplish, He makes it into another vessel. This can be seen in the rejection and crucifixion of Jesus.

Let us look at the crucifixion. Israel should be teaching and leading the nations of the world to worship the Messiah, but instead, they encouraged the people to shout, "crucify Him!" It is because they got spoiled in the Potter's hands, through their rebellion, that God used them for another purpose, which still brought Him glory. The Apostle Paul is now asking the Jew, who are being used for a different purpose, "Who are you to tell God how to use you? Who are you to tell God how to mold you or what to accomplish through you?" In essence, he is saying to that pot of clay which has been rebelling against God, "You have no right to tell God what to do."

The Apostle Paul goes on to note that the Gentiles have attained to the righteousness of God, because they pursued it by faith, but the Jews did not attain to it, because they sought it by works of the Law (Romans 9:30-32). In Romans 9:32-33, Paul tells us that the Jews stumbled over the stumbling stone. As it is written, "See, I lay in Zion a stone that causes people to stumble and a rock that makes them fall, and the one who believes in him will never be put to shame." This was quoted from Isaiah 28:16 and is a prophecy about the Messiah. This prophecy was fulfilled in Jesus, and that is why we see the majority of the leaders and teachers of the Jews rejecting Jesus as Messiah. However, "The stone that the builders rejected has become the cornerstone: The Lord has done this, and it is marvelous in our eyes" (Psalm 118:22-29).

In the verses that follow chapter 9:33, the Apostle Paul continues to express that his desire and prayer is for Israel to be saved. It may be that he had this desire to see the people saved, because that is the desire of God, as well. Something interesting is happening here though, because if the Apostle Paul believed, like the Determinist today, that those who were broken off were reprobates created for destruction from before the creation of the world, then he would not be praying for them, and holding out hope that they might be saved (Romans 10:1).

It is, therefore, clear that the Apostle Paul does not believe that these people were hopeless or cut off forever. He told us that they were blinded and cut off until God has accomplished His work of bringing in the Gentiles (Romans 11:25). He reinforces the point that the Jews did not submit to God's righteousness but sought to establish a righteous on their own.

They had zeal, but it was not according to the knowledge that comes from God. They did not recognize that the same Jesus whom they have crucified, who has been raised from the dead, is the end of the Law for righteousness (Romans 10:2-4). This is basically the same thought carried over from Romans 9:31-33.

10.4 How Does One Get Saved?

The Apostle Paul explains from Romans 10:9-15 how a person gets saved and receives righteousness from God. He tells us that the process is: a person hears the Gospel, believes, and confesses, after which that person is saved. He is making it clear in these verses that only after one believes that righteousness is given, and salvation is received. In the text, the only thing that needs to happen for the persons to believe is for a preacher to speak the life giving, soul piercing word of God. Faith comes by hearing the word of God, and that is why the Gospel is important (v 13-17). Everyone who hears the Gospel and trusts in God (call on the name of the Lord) shall be saved. The Apostle Paul tells us in verse 17 that faith comes by hearing the word of God. Therefore, he asks the question, "Did Israel not hear the message?"

He is asking this question, because since faith comes by hearing the message, and the Jews are not trusting in Christ, does that mean that they have not heard the message? NO! They are not being saved because they are rebelling against the message. They are being a pot or vessel that has gone spoiled. God says of His people Israel, "All day long I have held out my hands to a disobedient and obstinate people" (Romans 10:21).

Doesn't God seem sincere here? If God knew that He did not choose them for salvation, would it not be hypocritical and deceptive to act as if He wanted them to come?

Wayne Grudem (1994), in his systematic theology, posits that God must not be blamed for the sin of His creatures. However, Grudem also insists that it is God who ordained sin to come into the world (p, 492). Grudem cannot have it both ways. For example, he cannot claim that God ordained or decreed that His creatures sin, and then claim that the creatures are to be held accountable, for that which God determined them to do, and they could not have done otherwise.

Sproul (1986) does not flinch in his admittance of double predestination in his book *Chosen by God*. He says, "if there is such a thing as predestination at all, and if the predestination does not include all people, then we must not shrink from the necessary inference that there are two sides to predestination"(p. 141). Although I do not agree with Sproul's deterministic worldview, I totally agree with his statement here; because the same God who determined some for salvation, also determined the rest for damnation, if Determinism is true.

The term, "whosoever will may come," becomes meaningless, if the Creator has ordained that they cannot come, unless He gives them life that enables them to come. I will address this issue later, when we examine the doctrine on God's eternal decrees. For now, I want to say that God's offer and invitation to salvation looks very different from what Determinists tell us.

We read the last two verses in Romans 10, which are quoted from Isaiah 65. In verses 1-3 of Isaiah 65, it says:

> I revealed myself to those who did not ask for me; I was found by those who did not seek me. To a

nation that did not call on my name, I said, 'Here am I'. All day long I have held out my hands to an obstinate people, who walk in ways not good. Pursuing their own imaginations, a people who continually provoke me to my very face, offering sacrifices in gardens and burning incense on alters of brick.

The Apostle Paul then moved on in chapter 11 to re-emphasize the point that God has not totally rejected His people forever (v 1-3). He pointed to the fact that God had preserved those who did not worship Baal. These believers in the Old Testament remained true to God, when others had gone off into idol worship and syncretism. Israel attempted to mix the worship of the true God and that of the idols, which the other nations worshipped. This is why Elijah challenged the leaders and his people Israel, to stop limping between two opinions. He said to them, "How long will you waver between two opinions? If the Lord is God, follow Him, but if Baal is God, follow him" (1 Kings 18:21).

The Apostle Paul makes the point that he is an Israelite who trusted in Jesus Christ, which is evidence that God has not rejected His people (Romans 11:1). Elijah thought that he was the only prophet that had survived the onslaught of the persecutors who murdered God's servants. These prophets were chosen or elected to serve God by bringing the word of God to the people.

The Israelites sought earnestly to earn the righteousness of God, but they did not obtain it (Romans 11:7). The Apostle Paul then quoted David's imprecatory prayer. This type of prayer that calls for judgment or calamity against those who are in rebellion against God. This prayer is found in Psalm 69:22-23. All the Old

Testament passages that are quoted by Paul in verses 8-10, are speaking about people who were being judged because they are living in rebellion against God (Deuteronomy 29:4, Isaiah 29:10). Paul reminded the readers that they received the Spirit from God, when they believed the Gospel and not while they were doing the works of the Law (Galatians 3:5-6). God knew from the beginning that He was going to justify all people through the same means, and that is by grace through faith (Galatians 3:6-8). The Apostle Paul said, "So those who rely on faith are blessed along with Abraham, the man of faith" (Galatians 3:9). This was God's plan, to bless Abraham and make him a blessing to all the people of the world (Genesis 12:3).

Dr. Leighton Flowers puts it nicely in his book "The Potter's Promise" (2017) when he said, "God intended to cut off Israel and graft in the Gentiles. The potter has sovereignly orchestrated both the cutting off of Israel (by way of Judicial hardening) and the engrafting of the Gentiles (by way of the gospel appeal) in the climatic fulfillment of His promise to Abraham to bless all the families of the earth" (p. 146).

In Romans 11:11 the Apostle Paul says that Israel did not stumble that they might not recover, but that God's plan of bringing in the Gentiles might come to pass. This also has in it the purpose of making Israel jealous of how the Gentiles are now being called the people of God. The hope Paul has, is that by moving his people to jealousy some might come to Christ (v 14). He explains that the work that God is doing, is bringing His people Israel to their senses by revealing to them the Messiah they have been rejecting. He reminded them that those who are broken off, who are not trusting in Jesus as yet, God has them as His elect, according to the promise of God that He will use them to bring the Word to the world (v28). Do remember though, that only those who are of faith are true children of Abraham (Galatians 3:7).

We have examined the portion that the Apostle Paul addressed on the topic of Election, and we did not see any biblical evidence in chapters 9-11 in Romans that teach exhaustive divine determinism. We have not seen anything that suggests that God had chosen some people to salvation from before the foundation of the world, while leaving the majority of the people whom He had ordained for damnation before they were even born. The Scripture rightly interpreted, will never end in determinism. What we have seen in the text, is not a limiting of people to salvation, but an opening of the opportunity to Gentiles to receive salvation through faith in Jesus. God simply used rebellious Israel, who was being hardened at this time, as His instrument to accomplish His purpose of the crucifixion and the Gentiles being engrafted into the Kingdom of God.

In Christ Alone

In Ephesians 1:1-14, the Apostle Paul gives some important insights on election and its result. In this portion of Scripture, he is not telling us why we believed, but he is telling us what will happen to those who believe. Let us seek to answer some questions from the text.

Who Did the Choosing?

According to Ephesians 1:3-4, it is the Father who has done the choosing. The writer says, "Praise be to the God and Father of our Lord Jesus Christ, who has blessed us in the heavenly realms with every spiritual blessing in Christ. For He chose us in Him before the creation of the world to be blameless in His sight." We mentioned earlier, and it is quite fitting to state here again, that every spiritual blessing we have received or will receive is because of our connection to Christ. It is because we are in Christ, that we received all the spiritual blessings and inheritance that we will get later. He states clearly in the text, that the Father is the one who has done the choosing.

Who were Chosen?

The Apostle Paul is speaking to saints at Ephesus. He is telling them that they are chosen by the Father. He is not speaking to unsaved people and telling them how they can be saved. He is telling saved people that they are blessed with all spiritual blessings in heavenly places in Christ. This text is not about how the unsaved can be converted, but how the saints are blessed.

When Did God Make the Choice?

The Apostle Paul says that God the Father chose the saints in Christ from before the foundation of the world. This statement has caused a lot of difficulty for those who do not understand the significance of his use of the term "in Christ." In this passage of Scripture, along with many others, "being in Christ" is the ultimate reason for our blessings of inheritance and glorification, which is what the text is about. Some people constantly try to get this text to say what it does not say, by adding words to the text. For example, in verse 4, they will add the words (to be) so that it reads, "According as He has chosen us 'to be' in Him before the foundation of the world." However, that is not what the verse says. It does not say that the saints were chosen "to be" in Him (Jesus), but that they were chosen "IN HIM."

Others try another way of getting around what the text says, by misquoting the text. This group, however, does not add words to the text but subtract them. They render the verse like this, "according as He has chosen us before the foundation of the world." I hope you realize the essential element that they have left out. They have left out or subtracted "in Christ" from the text, which changes the meaning of the text entirely. Count for yourself how many times in this passage alone that Paul uses the phrase "in Christ" or "in Him" or "in whom." This is his emphasis, because the saints' inheritance, sanctification and glorification are in Christ.

10. 5
How Does Election Work?

Notice how the Apostle Paul uses the term "in Christ" in this passage of the Scripture, which is similar to how he uses it in other Epistles. He presents Jesus as an entity, into whom we must enter to receive the benefit of our connection to Him. Before I explain the use of this term "in Christ," I want to dispel the opinion of two alterations of the Ephesians 1:4 text mentioned earlier.

The adding of the words "to be" is not to be ignored as insignificant, because it changes the meaning of the text. What they are suggesting by this rendering, is that God has, from before the foundation of the world, chosen some unsaved people, who did not yet exist, to be converted. The first problem with this view, is that this passage is not speaking about unsaved people, nor is it focused on conversion to Jesus. The text mentions the blessings in verse 3, the inheritance and glorification in verses 13-14. Those that leave out the words "in Him" do as much damage as well as those who add "to be." The persons that insist that God has chosen unsaved people before the foundation of the world are not recognizing that God's elect in the text, are the saints and faithful in Christ Jesus. Therefore, as far as this text is concerned, there are no unsaved people chosen for glorification.

Let us look at further evidence why their view of God choosing the unsaved to salvation from before the creation, does not fit the text. The Apostle Paul himself tells us when they were put in Christ. The text says, "That we should be to the praise of His glory who first trusted in Christ. In whom you also trusted, after that ye heard the word of truth, the gospel of your salvation in whom also after that ye believed, ye were sealed with that Holy Spirit of promises (Ephesians 1:12-13, KJV). Please note the sequence here. They heard the Gospel (v13). They believed the Gospel (v13). They were then sealed with the Holy Spirit (v 13). They are awaiting their glorification which includes the redemption of their bodies (v 14).

It means therefore, that the believers were not saved from before the foundation of the world. Nor were they in Christ before the world was created. 1 Corinthians tells us, "For by one Spirit we were all baptized into one body, whether we be Jews or Gentiles, whether we be bond or free; and have been all made to drink into one Spirit" (1 Corinthians 12:13, KJV). If the people were already in Christ before they trusted in Christ for salvation, how are they now being put into Christ when they believe? Note, no unsaved is being put into Christ in any of these texts.

Furthermore, there are other problems with the view that the unsaved was in Christ before the creation of the world. The Apostle Paul already tells us in 1 Corinthians 8:12 and Ephesians 1:13 that they were put into Christ when they believed. Now look at what he says in Ephesians 2:12-13, "Remember that at that time you were separate from Christ, excluded from the citizenship in Israel and foreigners to the covenants of the Promise, without hope and without God in the world." He is speaking to the Gentile Christians, reminding them of who they were before they trusted in Jesus Christ for salvation.

Please note that before they trusted Christ they were separated from Christ, without hope and without God. Therefore, these believers were not in Christ, and at the same time outside of God. This text is so clear that someone would have to try hard to miss it. Another question to ask is, according to those who believe that the unsaved were chosen to be saved from before the world was created, before he was even born; how did he come out of Christ at birth? How were they sinners who need to trust Christ for salvation and to be put back into Christ? This would have to be the case because he was not born a saint in Christ. He would need to trust Christ like anyone else to be saved. However, if he were already in Christ and then at birth fell out of Christ and became a sinner, by what means did he get back into Christ? Where is it said in Scripture that people fell out of Christ because they were born sinners and therefore separated from God?

The view that God chose unsaved people before the foundation of the world to be saved, and therefore they were in Christ before the world was created is false. Let me give you one more reason. The Apostle Paul in Galatians 4:7-9 says, "So you are no longer a slave, but God's child; and since you are His child,

God has made you also an heir. Formally, when you did not know God, you were slaves to those who by nature are not gods. But now that you know God, or rather are known by God, how is it that you are turning back to those weak and miserable forces? Do you wish to be enslaved by them all over again?" Paul is telling us clearly that there was a time when the Galatians did not know God. He also makes it plain that there was a time when God did not know them. How could he say that the All-Knowing God did not know them?

Here, Paul is not speaking about God's omniscience, but God's relationship with the people. He is not saying that God was unaware of them before, and they have now come to His knowledge. Instead, Paul is using the word "know" as it was often used in that time to speak of an intimate relationship. For example, Jesus says to us in Scripture that many are going to come in the end, claiming all the good deeds they have done in His name. He will say to them plainly, "I never knew you. Away from me, you evildoers" (Matthew 7:23). This is in reference to the time of judgment when Jesus will pronounce judgment on those who are not connected to Him. Of course, Jesus knew who they were; He just did not have an intimate relationship with them, which only comes through faith in Him. Since God did not know the Galatians before they became Christians, it is clear evidence that they were not in Christ before the foundation of the world.

Here is a text that is important to this point. Romans 16:7 says, "Greet Andronicus and Junica, my fellow Jews who have been in prison with me. They are outstanding among the Apostles, and they were in Christ before I was." This is the final dagger to the heart of the view that Christians were in Christ from before the creation of the world. Notice that after he mentioned the two Jewish believers, Andronicus and Junica, he said that they were in Christ before he was. This would mean that all believers are not put in Christ at the same time, or else he could not say that these believers were in Christ before him. If people were put into Christ before the world was created, then all believers would have been in Christ before the world was. There are too many problems with that view, and Scripture has proven that it is false. Our salvation is not predicated on election but on faith in Christ. The Elect are the "in Christ ones."

Let us look at how the election works. Since Christ is the elect of God (Isaiah 42:1, Matthew 12:18, 1 Peter 2:4, Luke 23:35), those who are in Him are also seen as chosen. In the same way we understand that we have no righteousness of our own, because all our righteousness is as filthy rags (Isaiah 64:6). Nevertheless, the Apostle Paul says in 2 Corinthians 5:21 that we are the righteousness of God in Christ. We are seen as righteous before God because we are in Christ. He has put on our account which was bankrupt, the righteousness, blessings, riches in glory, and has made us joint heirs with Christ (Romans 8:16-17).

The reason it is said that the saints were chosen "in Christ" before the foundation, is because Christ, The Eternal One, The Elect, existed before the world was created. He, "The Entity," was chosen and because we are now in Him, we are also considered the chosen as well. I think we have presented enough evidence, that apart from Jesus Christ, we are not chosen in this sense.

10.6
What are they Chosen to do?

In Christ, the believers were chosen to live a sanctified life empowered by the Holy Spirit. Ephesians 1:4 says that they were chosen "to be holy and blameless in His sight." It is evident in Scripture that Christians are not only chosen for blessings, inheritance, and glorification, but for service as well. There are some duties that God has prepared for us to accomplish. The Apostle Paul says in Ephesians 2:10, "For we are God's handiwork, created in Christ Jesus to do good works, which God prepared in advance for us to do."

There are many passages in Scripture that mention persons chosen for service. The word elect simply means to choose; it does not mean to save. Jacob was chosen, not to be saved, but to serve as the son through whose line the Messiah would come. His line was supposed to be the mouthpiece for God, who would carry the message of the Messiah to the nations of the world. Edom (Esau) was chosen to serve Israel (Jacob) and they did not. Too many times people interpret the term chose as saved.

As we showed earlier, there are several people in Scripture who were chosen to do God's will. Some of them God used in their rebellion to accomplish His purpose, like Joseph's brothers, Pharaoh, and the Jewish leaders and people who crucified Christ. God accomplished His plan of deliverance even through their deeds. Since God is Sovereign, He can intervene in a situation and stop the evil that is about to happen if that serves His purpose. For example, when King Herod had planned to kill Peter, God delivered Peter from prison the night before, because God had other things that He wanted to accomplish through Peter (Acts 12:3-19). The wise men were guided by the Lord to go another way and not return to Herod who was plotting to kill baby Jesus (Matthew 2:12). Joseph's brothers wanted to kill him. God intervened because He had a plan to be accomplished in Egypt, where Joseph was eventually taken (Genesis 50:20).

We also see Jonah who was chosen for service. This was to bring the word of God to a wicked people who God wanted to save. Jonah resisted, but God proved that He has power over man. God demonstrated that He can and does overrule in situations as it pleases Him. Notice though, that although God overpowered Jonah's acts of rebellion, Jonah's mind and will for the people of Nineveh was not changed. Jonah, at the end of the book was angry with God for saving the people who repented (Jonah 3:10).

This text proves that God can overrule in a situation and have His way, without the person's will being changed. In a similar way, you might intervene when your elder child beat up on your younger child. The elder child might still want to beat up the younger child because his mind has not changed, but he is prevented from doing so. Therefore, it is a fact that God can overrule and overpower someone without changing their will, just like He did with Jonah.

Finally, I want to show you the way the Apostle Paul presents the position and privilege that we have because we are in Christ. Colossians 3:1-4 says,

> Since then, you have been raised with Christ, set your hearts on things above, where Christ is, seated at the right hand of God. Set your minds on things above, not on earthly things. For you died,

and your life is now hidden with Christ in God. When Christ, who is your life, appears, then you also will appear with Him in glory." So, all the glory, blessings and inheritance of being heir that we will receive is because we are now in Christ. Our status and transfer are from death to life. Christ is our life, and we have no life and glory outside of Him.

He mentions in verse 4, that we will appear with Christ in glory, when Christ who is our life appears.

This is similar to what the Apostle John was looking forward to when he said that there is coming a day in the future when our full redemption will be manifested, and we will be like Jesus (1 John 3:1-2). Galatians 3:26-27 says, "So in Christ Jesus you are all children of God through faith, for all you who were baptized into Christ have clothed yourself with Christ." Only those who become children of God through faith, have been put into Christ through the baptism by the Holy Spirit (1Corinthians 12:13). It is Christ in you that is the hope of glory (Colossians 1:27). In Christ, you who believe are the chosen of God.

Questions to Contemplate/Discuss

a. Who does the choosing in Ephesians 1?
b. Who are the Chosen?
c. When were they Chosen?
d. Explain how it works

CHAPTER 11:
God's Sovereignty

In this chapter, our focus is on defending the character of God. We believe that the Scripture makes it abundantly clear that God is holy, righteous, powerful, and loving. These attributes are in the very nature of God. Before anything was created in the whole universe, before there were angels, planets or people; God is holy, righteous, powerful, and loving. Love was shared in the Godhead between Father, Son, and the Holy Spirit before time began.

II. 1 What is the Meaning of Sovereignty?

God's Sovereignty speaks of His right to rule as He pleases. The Sovereign in Scripture is the King. This is used in reference to God when the text says Lord. For example, Psalm 135:5-6 says, "I know that the Lord is great, that our Lord is greater than all gods. The Lord does whatever pleases Him, in the heavens and on the earth, in the seas and all their depths." We also read in Psalm 115:3, "Our God is in heaven; He does whatever pleases Him." Verse 16 of this same chapter says, "The highest heavens belong to the Lord, but the earth he has given to mankind."

When we have a clear understanding of what the word Sovereign means, we will be better able to see God in the way Scripture presents Him. As in all other context or dictionary, the Bible presents sovereignty as the King's right to rule His domain as He wills. Notice in the verse above where it says that God has given the earth to men, this does not mean that God no longer owns the universe, nor does it mean that God cannot overrule what man is doing in the earth. It does mean however, that God has chosen to rule in a way that allows His creatures a level of autonomy.

II. 2 The Manifestation of God's Sovereignty

God gave mankind the right to rule or have dominion in the earth, according to Genesis 1:28-29. However, when Adam and Eve disobeyed God's command, God overruled in the situation and threw them out of the Garden (Genesis 3:24). Tony Evans in his book "The Kingdom Agenda" makes the same point when he said "God has appointed us as managers or stewards of His kingdom in this age. And some day we will rule with Him in the ultimate expression of His kingdom in the millennial reign of Jesus Christ on earth." Evans (1999) goes on to state that mankind was created and appointed a place of service in God's kingdom to demonstrate His glory, His power, and His ultimate triumph to all of creation (p.49). So, although God gave human beings a certain amount of authority, He still holds the right to intervene when things do not go the way He intended. God gave His creation the power and autonomy to have dominion in the earth. He has the right to give power to people if He wills, since He is God and does what He pleases; or is that not something God is free to do?

Another passage that turns Determinism on its head is 1 Corinthians 10:13. Let me explain what I mean. The text says, "No temptation has overtaken us except what is common to mankind. And God is faithful; He will not let you be tempted beyond what you can bear. But when you are tempted, He will also provide a way out so that you can bear it." According to this verse, the Christian does not have to sin when he is tempted because the faithful God has provided a way of escape for him.

Therefore, if the Christian sins, it is because he did not take the way of escape that God had provided for him. This truth of Scripture clearly contradicts both hard Determinism and Compatibilism. Let me show you why. They claim that all things happen because God decreed it; but God did not decree His children to sin. The verse is clear that God wants his children to escape the temptation, and has provided the means for them to do so. Since that is true, it must also be true that they have libertarian free will, since they are able to choose the opposite of what God wills for them.

It is the Sovereign God who has given individuals the ability to obey or to not obey. We addressed in an earlier chapter that when God hardened the heart of Pharaoh, and the Jews who crucified Jesus, they were already rebelling against God's will. For us to get a good appreciation of the manifestation of God's Sovereignty, we need to bear in mind what it means to be Sovereign. It simply means that God has the right to rule as he pleases. The crucial question though is, how does God want to rule? Before the fall of Lucifer (a very powerful angel who became Satan) and his followers; before the fall of Adam and Eve, God gave them some level of freedom which is still evident in the world today.

It seems, therefore, that the Sovereign Lord saw it fit to give His creation, such as angels and human beings, the power to choose, even though He knew that they would choose against His Will. Lucifer was able to choose to sin against God even though he was created sinless. Adam and Eve were also created sinless, but they also chose to sin against God (Genesis 3:6-7). Neither Lucifer, (who became the devil), nor Adam and Eve, had any "sin nature" that would have caused them to have a corruption in their very being that leaves them with a predisposition towards sin. Unless someone is brave enough to say that God is the One who caused them to sin by His eternal decrees or preordained them to fall, we need to just admit that it was the creatures' choice, because they were free to obey or to disobey.

We want to ask, then, in light of the fact that God created Lucifer and the other angels, and Adam and Eve, and gave them the power to make choice; was He still Sovereign at that time? If God was Sovereign when He gave them the ability to choose for themselves? Did He lose that sovereignty (right to rule as He pleases) when they fell? No! God is still Sovereign King of heaven and earth. He gets to choose how He wants to rule, which seems to be giving some autonomy to His creatures to make free choices.

Now, let me explain what I mean by freedom. I am not speaking of the ability to do whatever the heart desires, because it was a freedom within boundaries. For example, Lucifer wanted to rule God's throne. However, he was cast out by the True Ruler; who is Sovereign. In chapters 1 and 2 of the Book of Job, we also see where God gave Satan a certain amount of freedom and autonomy to inflict Job and his family with pain and problems, but it was within boundaries set by God. The fact that we have the right to choose does not mean that we can cause whatever we desire to happen. Nor does it mean that we decide the consequences of our actions. So, the King of the universe allows some level of autonomy, but He decides the consequences or rewards for our actions. Adam and Eve experienced this fact the day they sinned. God had warned them that in the day they eat of the forbidden fruit, they will die. They ate nevertheless. So, God, the King, determined the penalty when the creature committed the sin (Genesis 3).

By freedom, therefore, I mean libertarian freedom. By the way, that is the only real freedom in the true sense of the word. Libertarian freedom is the ability to choose something and also not to choose that thing. In other words, it is the ability to choose 'A' and also not to choose 'A'. Therefore, the agent himself is making the choice for a particular action, but he could have chosen otherwise. If this kind of freedom does not exist, then we cannot make sense of the fall of Lucifer, or Adam, or Eve. The real questions are, did God lose His Kingship after the fall? Has He lost His Sovereignty or right to rule as He pleases? In light of evidence in Scripture I must say no, He has not.

Questions to Contemplate/Discuss

a. What does the word Sovereign mean?
b. Did God stop being Sovereign after the fall of His creatures?
c. Explain why 1 Corinthians 10:13 refutes Determinism.

CHAPTER 12:

Compatibilism?

12. I
What is Compatibilism?

We will now be launching an attack on Theistic Determinism. The main view we want to contend with is the idea that everything that happens in the universe, whether good or evil, is determined by God. Compatibilists insist that even the wickedness that people do is decreed by God, yet He holds them accountable for the evils He decrees for them to do. According to Compatibilists, man's thoughts and actions are all determined by God. Compatibilism is often referred to as soft determinism because of its distinction regarding the creature's responsibility. The hard Determinist holds that because all things are determined by God, and He is the only Person who has libertarian freedom, then all other beings are not free. Therefore, they are not responsible for their behavior. This view makes it plain that all blame and praise go to God.

It is very important to note that Compatibilists are Determinists, but they believe that determinism and freedom to choose are compatible. The Compatibilists want to give God all the glory for both good and evil events in the universe because it was so determined by God, but they refuse to blame God for the evil He determines for men and angels to do. I know at this point you are saying that their view is a bit confusing, I agree, but let me explain how they arrived at that point.

Compatibilists recognize that if they say all things are determined by God, including all sinful actions, while maintaining that only God has libertarian freedom. This would put the blame of our sinful thoughts and behavior on God. This is not something they are willing to tolerate; therefore, they redefined freedom in a way that will get God off the hook for the evils they claim He determined for mankind and angels to do. This redefinition of freedom does not help their case one bit. The moment someone understands the meaning they have proposed for freedom and see its implication, the contradiction and confusion emerge. If we desire truth, we are to reject contradictions.

Geisler and Bocchino (2001) concur, as they emphasized in their book "Unshakable Foundations" that the fundamental principle of logic is the law of non-contradiction. They insist that it is the most powerful logical principle you can learn. They also show how potent this law is by demonstrating that one has to use it in one's attempt to deny it. Let's look at their example: "if someone were to say, 'I deny the law of non-contradiction' it would be the opposite of saying 'I affirm the law of non-contradiction'. In the very act of denying the law of non-contradiction the person must use it" (P, 23). Therefore, this law must be respected because there is no meaningful communication without it in its rightful place.

Therefore, what we claim as true must not contradict reality. J. P. Moreland, in his description of truth, says "truth is a relation of correspondence between a thought and the world. If a thought really describes the world accurately, it is true" (1987, p.81-82). This means that if a statement does not match that to which it refers, it is certainly not true. It must match or correspond with the reality to which it refers.

12. 2
Is Compatibilism Supported by the Bible?

Compatibilists have redefined freedom to mean a person doing what he/she wants to do. Freedom for the Compatibilist is reduced to animal instinct. It's just like a shark that craves meat. Therefore, no one has to force it to eat meat because that is what it wants to do. However, here is where I have a major issue with the language of the Compatibilist, they refuse to make plain what they are proposing. Persons who are ignorant of what Determinists teach about God's eternal Decree will continue to be drawn to their doctrine until it is stated plainly what they really mean by the words they use. They continue to emphasize that an individual wants what he/she wants and therefore does what he/she wants. This they claim, without clearly stating why the individual wants to do what he/she does.

On soft determinism (Compatibilism), they believe that as long as the person is not being forced / coerced on the outside to influence their behavior, then they are acting freely, because they are doing what they desire to do. The real question is this, who gave them those desires? They insist that there is no logical contradiction between the claim that all the thoughts, desires, and actions are determined by God, and people are responsible for those actions. They believe that their redefinition of freedom which is a meaning that is foreign to the concept of freedom in any other system or dictionary. It gives them a way of escape from the serious implication of God being culpable for the sins He causes people to do. There is no escape, because although the man does what he wants to do, it is God working on the inside of the individual that causes him to want what he wants, and therefore did what he wants to do because he is determined on the inside by God to do it, according to Compatibilism.

If it is true that God is the only person who has the ability to think or chose freely, then no amount of nice sounding language can be used to remove culpability from Him, since He is the One who is determining our wants, which ultimately determines our actions. The Compatibilists want to have it both ways. If the desires that people have are given to them on the inside by God, then they don't need to be forced by anyone or anything on the outside, because they are already fixed inwardly by God, who will later condemn them for wanting what He has put in them to want and do.

If this sounds confusing or contradicting to you, that's because it is. The moment the ambiguity is removed, the escape route is removed, and we can see clearly the negative picture they have presented of God. Don't be dismayed; the Compatibilist's view does not reflect the God or freedom evidenced in Scripture.

God is still in control even though He does not stop every sinful act from happening. He has the knowledge, wisdom, and power to work all things together for good and accomplish His glory. How could Determinists truly believe that individuals are responsible for their sinful actions, when those thoughts and desires are determined by God? Compatibilists believe that God determines or causes every thought or acts of mankind, yet mankind is still responsible for the things God determines or causes him to do. They teach that God decrees or causes all things that come to pass in the universe. This includes all the wickedness we see in the world. The torture and murder of millions of people, the rape and murder of a five-month-old child and the most heinous evils one can imagine. Their claim is a very extraordinary claim, one which requires sufficient evidence from Scripture. This is crucial because their claim impugns the character of God. For example, the claim that nothing happens in the universe except by God's decree is putting the blame on God for all the evils His creatures do.

Although the Sovereign God gives the right to choose, He is not pleased with the thoughts and actions that go against His Will. Clearly, God was displeased with Lucifer and some of the angels, along with Adam and Eve, who all rebelled. Therefore, God punished them for their rebellion. It would be a crazy kind of God, who caused them to rebel and then judged them for rebelling. Another point that is worth mentioning here, is that no reasonable person would get upset with a man who has no hands or feet, if he did not obey a command to run a 10 k marathon.

For us to get a good appreciation of the matter we are discussing, we need to bear in mind what it means to be Sovereign. It means that God has the right to rule as He pleases. The question then is, how does He choose to rule? Before the fall of Lucifer and his angels; before the fall of Adam and Eve, God gave them some level of freedom which is still evident in the world today. Ephesians 6:12 says, "For our struggle is not against flesh and blood, but against the rulers, against the authorities, against the powers of this dark world and against spiritual forces of evil in the heavenly realms."

Therefore, it seems evident to me that God, the Sovereign King, has given some level of autonomy in the world for His creatures to rule, yet not without limits. The fact that God intervenes in some situation to change the course of things proves that God's will is not always done in the earth. Jesus taught His disciples to pray to God the Father saying, "Your will be done on earth as it is in heaven" (Matthew 6:10). If God's will is always done, then this prayer does not make sense, since the request is for God's will to be done in earth, as it is done in heaven.

In an effort to escape the grip of this truth, some argue that there is no contradiction in asserting that God's will is always done, because God has two wills. They make a distinction between God's Revealed Will in Scripture and His Secret Decretive Will. What they go on to describe is a clear contradiction. It is like saying 'A' is not 'A'. It is like mentioning a bachelor who is married. That type of philosophy will cause their doctrine to crash in a load of contradiction. For example, a bachelor, by definition is an unmarried man. So, when that is understood, it should be clear to all that the bachelor is not married. It is important to note that opposite truth claims cannot be true at the same time and in the same sense. In other words, if the claim that Jimmy is a bachelor is true, then to also state that he is a married man must be false. Jimmy might become a married man tomorrow, but he is a bachelor until he is married.

Let us now consider what the Determinists are asking us to believe. In essence, they are saying that the explicit, Revealed Will of God in the Bible is not God's real Will. They teach that although God commands people to not indulge in sexual sins, it is His Secret Decretive Will that they do sin, because nothing happens without God willing it to happen. This, however, seems to go totally against Scripture. For example, 1 Thessalonians 4:34 says, "It is God's will that you should be sanctified, that you should avoid sexual immorality, that each of you should learn to control your own body in a way that is holy and honourable." The author continues in verse 7-8 saying, "For God did not call us to be impure, but to live a holy life. Therefore, anyone who rejects this instruction does not reject a human being but God; the very God who gives us the Holy Spirit."

Is it not clear in these verses that God's Will is for His people to live holy and keep themselves from being polluted by their sinful passions? But it is a fact, though, that we all at some point became polluted by our own sinful desires and deeds. When we sin against His clearly stated Will, are we to maintain that we are doing God's Secret Decretive Will? That is absurd! The Apostle Paul also tells us in Ephesians 2:10, "For we are God's handiwork created in Christ Jesus to do good works which God prepared in advance for us to do." When we refuse to do the good works that God has prepared for us to do, are we still doing His Secret Decretive Will? How can we know when God's clearly revealed Will in Scripture is not really what He wants to happen? By the way, in the view of the Determinist, only the things God decrees come to pass, which includes all the evil in the world.

There is a difference in stating that God has two wills which do not contradict each other. For example, God wants all men to repent and come to the knowledge of the truth, for it is not His Will that any should perish, but that all should come to repentance (2 Peter 3:9). He also wills that man would choose His gracious offer of salvation which was provided for everyone. So, although God's Will is that all would come and be saved, His Will to give man the ability to choose, will affect how many will come. Therefore, God's Will to give freedom of choice to mankind is an addition to His Will of wanting everyone to be saved. It would be a contradiction to claim that God wills that everyone be saved, and that He also wills that only some individuals be saved. This type of speech makes no sense because it would mean that the Bible is not good enough to tell us God's true Will and Desire.

In an earlier chapter, we already looked at biblical evidence of persons in Scripture who rebelled against the Will of God (Luke 7:30). I am not saying that God has not decreed some things, but I am sure on the biblical evidence, that He has not decreed or preordained all things that come to pass in the world. I understand that the main reason why the Determinists insist that God causes everything to come to pass is because they want to show God's power and control. However, in their effort to give all the glory to God and show Him as all powerful, they have ascribed to God, without even realizing an evil character, and therefore a weak characterization of God.

Let us consider the evidence for my claim from Scripture. Jeremiah 19:3-5, proves to us that God's Will is not always done in the earth. God pronounced judgment on the people because they did things that were against His Will. Verse 5 says, "They have built the high places of Baal to burn their children in the fire as offering to Baal, something I did not command or mention, nor did it enter my mind." In what way was this God's secret decretive will? No way! God did not command it. This means that it was not God's Revealed Will for them to do that thing. Nor was it God's Secretive Decretive Will, because He did not mention it privately to any Determinist, nor was it even in the Mind of God. When God said that it did not even come to His mind, He is not saying that He did not know that the people would do it, but that He had no intention or desire for them to do it. I know the view that God's Will is always done in the earth, is in the mind of the Determinist, but it is not in the mind of God or the word of God.

When a person sins, he sins because he is drawn away by his own lustful desires, according to James 1:13-15. Therefore, James warns that people should refuse from blaming God for their temptation and sin; since He cannot be tempted, nor does He tempt anyone to sin. Furthermore, there are things listed in Scripture that are in the world and they do not come from God. For example, the Apostle John tells us that, "The lust of the flesh, the lust of the eyes, and the pride of life, come not from the Father but from the world" (1 John 2:16). These verses in the Bible clearly state that pride and lust come from the world system, and not from God. We must not claim that God does things which the Scriptures clearly state that He does not do.

At this point the Determinist tries to evade the clear biblical conclusion, by claiming that God's foreknowledge of the events actually brings them to pass or cause them to be. Please note, that in their system, what they truly believe, is not that God allows evil events to happen and then redeem it in the end, but that God brings it to pass through His own Decretive Will. To foreknow does not mean to fore ordain. His knowledge is not causative. God knows the future because He is omniscient; not because He is causing the evil He knows about. For example, Jesus knew that Peter was going to deny him three times in one night, but Jesus did not cause Peter to deny Him. Jesus warned about the sin that Peter was going to commit but did not cause Peter to sin.

Here is an example of God's omniscience which did not prove causative. 1 Samuel 23:10-13 highlights a situation where David was on the run because he was being persecuted by King Saul. David heard that Saul was coming to the town in which he was hiding, so David prayed to God for insight and information. David said,

> LORD, God of Israel, your servant has heard definitely that Saul plans to come to Keilah and destroy the town on account of me. Will the citizens of Keilah surrender me to him? Will Saul come down, as your servant has heard? LORD, God of Israel, tell your servant. And the LORD said, 'he will.' Again, David asked, 'Will the citizens of Keilah surrender me and my men to Saul?' and the LORD said, 'they will.'

Here is a situation where God knows something, but His knowledge of the thing did not cause the thing to happen. David after hearing from God departed from the town, and when Saul heard that David fled the town, he did not go to the town. Notice, if David had stayed, then Saul would come to the town and the people would give up both David and his men to Saul. However, none of what God knew would happen if David had stayed actually happened in that situation, because His omniscience is not fore-ordination.

Those who insist that God can only know future events because He is the One causing them, are going against the biblical revelation. One of the texts that Determinists like to use to argue their point on this subject is Acts 4:27-31. We discussed this passage earlier, but it is fitting that we address something here. The Apostle Peter is not suggesting that God caused the people who are mentioned, to sin. He only points out that God determined beforehand that His Son would die for the sins of mankind on a cross at Calvary. The giving of the Son was the Father's choice. Then, Jesus chose to give His life as a ransom for sin.

Therefore, God used wicked men in their wickedness to accomplish the crucifixion. God did not make Pilate, Herod, and all the people to do evil. These people were already evil. The devil got into Judas (Luke 22:3), and Judas betrayed Jesus which was a part of the process and also foretold in prophecy. Judas was used for this purpose because the Lord knew that he loved money and he was also a thief (John 12:5-6). The Lord had to hide some things from the wicked leaders in order to get the crucifixion fulfilled. For if those leaders knew who Jesus really was, 'They would not have crucified the Lord of Glory" (1 Corinthians 2:8).

Here again, we see that God knew of something that would happen if the circumstances had been different. Therefore, what God knew would happen, if they had known the Messiah did not happen because it was hidden from their eyes so that the crucifixion could be accomplished. We must, therefore, exercise prudence as we distinguish between what God did, and what He allowed mankind to do, even in the crucifixion event. God gave His Son; the Son gave His life, and wicked men did evil which only accomplished the plan of God.

The God of the Bible often put the responsibility on the people to act in a way that is pleasing to Him. This is why He holds them accountable. A two-month-old girl child would not be held accountable for pooping in her diaper, even if I told her not to poop in her diaper. Common sense would suggest that, although I might say to her in the morning with much pleading and promises, "Please do not poop in your diaper" I would not be surprised when I see her diaper soiled later. Now, if you come to my house and saw me shouting at my two-month-old baby for pooping in her diaper, wouldn't you think that something is wrong with me? Would you not think that because you know she is not able to respond to my promises and pleas to not poop in her diaper? However, when she gets older and is able to understand, the accountability changes, because she is now responsible for not pooping in her pants.

When Compatibilists say that God is not causing the people to do evil when He determined all things to come to pass, they claim that it is because He is acting as an Author. This view, however, does nothing to help the Compatibilist to get God off the hook for causing evil. Let's imagine the author of the book, Friday the 13th. Would it make sense to you, if at the end of the movie you hear the author accusing Jason who is the evil person in the movie of being too wicked or cruel? Wouldn't it amaze you since the wickedness of Jason came from the pen of the author? Jason only did what he was scripted to do; his actions were already determined before the movie began by the pen of the author.

Please notice that in the movie or the novel, the author is the one who determines, or decrees whatsoever comes to pass. Those who use this analogy to claim that the actors are free to do or to not do the decree of the author, are not being consistent with the Compatibilist world view. Furthermore, the author of a book does not truly represent the Compatibilist view because the characters are not real. However, if the characters are real people, who are determined from the inside to want to act in an evil manner, then the "Author" (God) who determines their desires is culpable for their behavior.

To insist that God uses secondary means to accomplish these evil actions does not get Him off the hook either. For example, when Uriah was killed, David was not near the battlefield, but he was the criminal as far as God is concerned. God, through His prophet Nathan, accused David of killing Uriah to get his wife Bathsheba (2 Samuel 12:9). The army was used by David to accomplish his evil plan through Joab, but God said that David was the murderer.

If God is really the One behind the scenes determining people's thoughts, desires and actions that affects and determines what they want and do, then God is the culprit behind the evils committed in the world. We are so happy that, that view does not represent the God of the Bible. An important note in this issue is that the consistent Determinist recognizes that his system demands that all choices and desires are determined by God. This includes the food we eat, the friends we keep, the clothes we wear, the things we fear, the things we buy, and when we lie. It's all determined by God in their worldview.

There are so many problems with Compatibilism that I am not sure where to stop. In order to reject true freedom as it is presented in Scripture and anywhere else that does not hold to Determinism, they have to redefine it. When their teaching is stated clearly it becomes very absurd to the thinking person. This is why Compatibilists do not use plain language in explaining their position to anyone who is not already a Determinist. I am convinced that if many persons knew exactly what was being taught by the Compatibilist they would run as far away as possible from that system of Determinism. The fact that I am making plain what they believe and teach on their system about the character of God will be resented by Determinists because they know that the plain teaching of their worldview is very unpalatable, and obnoxious to the unsuspecting listener. Although they might be offended by the plain description of their doctrine of Determinism, they cannot clearly show where their view is misrepresented.

12.3
Making it Plain: Determinism Laid Bare

If the ambiguity is taken out of the way, Determinism will be gone as well. Can we really take God seriously with His offer of salvation? I have noticed over the years that whenever Determinism is plainly explained, people usually run from it.

Should we not believe God when He says that whoever will, may come? (Revelation 22:17); Yes, we can, and we should! The role of Evangelism in any system that holds to a deterministic worldview becomes meaningless. For example, how can Compatibilists proclaim in a sincere way that God's invitation is real? That can only be a true statement for Compatibilists if they really believe that anyone can come if they so choose. However, by using unclear language, Compatibilists are able to deceive the naïve listener into thinking that the invitation is real to all who are listening.

Let me explain what I mean by that. When Compatibilists share the Gospel, they are not being forthright in declaring exactly what is meant when they say whoever will, may come. They are not telling the listeners that they really believe that the listeners cannot come if they are not an elect. They are not telling the listeners that if they are not the elect they won't want to come unless God fixes their wants from the inside by regenerating them first. They are not telling the listeners that if God does not first regenerate them, they cannot want to come, no matter how many preaching they hear. They are not telling the listeners that only those who God has picked for salvation from before the foundation of the world can come. They are not telling their listeners not to worry, because if they are already chosen, they cannot refuse to come, because their desires have been fixed to want God.

The main reason why Compatibilism has the kind of following it now has is because Determinism is not usually explained in their evangelism. The normal Gospel is presented to win people to Christ, and then the Compatibilist teaches Determinism to nurture them into the system by presenting it as the true Gospel, which you can only see and understand after you have been drafted for salvation and into their community.

It is time to look at what the true Gospel of Scripture says. John 3:16 says, "For God so loved the world that he gave His one and only Son, that whoever believes in Him shall not perish but have everlasting life." The following verse tells us the reason for which Jesus was sent into the world by the Father. Jesus came not to condemn the world, but that through Him the world might be saved. God sounds very sincere by this offer. It really seems as if whoever comes to Him will receive life. At this point we need to consider if the Compatibilist's Determinism matches what the Gospel says.

Determinists believe that they should obey the command to evangelize, but they cannot truly look at any person and tell them that God loves them, or that they can receive the free gift of salvation. The reason they cannot honestly tell anyone that is because their doctrine, if practiced consistently, forbids them to. Since they do not know who the "elect" are, and only the elect can come and receive the offer of salvation, they will do a grave injustice to those people who actually believe that they are able to believe in Christ. What if someone believes their view on election and total depravity, and decides to live that out practically? Can you imagine how that would look?

In other words, if a man says that he is not concerned about whether he goes to heaven or hell because if he is one of the "elect" nothing can stop him or her from going to heaven, and if he is not an "elect," then nothing can stop him/her from going to hell, should Determinists blame him for thinking that way? What if the person says that he is just waiting for the Lord to call his name and wake him/her from the dead like Lazarus, should they call that individual stupid? If Determinists are consistent in their worldview, that is a reasonable position for the man/woman to take, since he can see nothing, hear nothing, and do nothing until he is given that life from God.

It is important to note that the Determinists' worldview does not offer any comfort of assurance to the non-elect or those who believe they are elect. Let's reason this matter together. The Gospel is Good News in Scripture, but it is not good news in Determinism. Compatibilists and hard Determinists know that the Gospel is not good news for the non- elect, because the non-elect cannot receive the gracious gift that is freely offered by God. The Gospel only serves to damn them even more, by piling more judgment and condemnation for not receiving the offer, which by the way, they could not receive because of God's Eternal Decree. Their rejection of the Gospel is caused by God's refusal to give them life to awaken them to receive eternal life in Christ. There goes the contradiction and confusing language again.

The Gospel then, is not good news for the "non- elect." However, it is not good news for those who think that they are elect either. Remember that in the Determinists' worldview, no one really knows who the "elect" are, and they will not know unless the professing believer perseveres to the end. With this in mind, consider a man who may have professed Christianity for thirty years, and tried to remain faithful to the end of his life. If that person does not make it to heaven because he was not one of the chosen, was the Gospel Good News for him? If he was deceived into thinking that he could just believe the Gospel and be saved, only to find out in the end that he was not chosen for salvation from before the foundation of the world, in what way was the Gospel Good News for him?

Furthermore, since no Determinist who is a professing Christian knows for sure that he is one of the elect, and since he cannot know until he dies and meets Jesus who will decide his destination, in what way can he be assured of heaven? The Determinists' view of election offers them no comfort or assurance because they cannot be sure that they are in that number of the "elect."

I reject Compatibilism because it is a system that is plagued with contradictions. You should reject the idea that God will do the logically impossible. Some Compatibilists claim that believing that God does the logically impossible things brings Him more glory. We will prove that that claim is nonsense.

I can declare right now that there are many things that God cannot do because He is God. I can get smarter, but God cannot. I can get stronger, but God cannot. I can tell a lie, but God cannot. The fact that I can get better, and God cannot, does not make God weaker. God cannot get any better, because His goodness cannot be improved upon, nor does it decrease. We should refuse the nice sounding words that claim to make God more glorious by ascribing to Him the ability to do the logically impossible.

If, by definition, an Eternal Being has no beginning of existence or ending of existence, it follows that God cannot make another Eternal Being. This is true because God would be bringing the being into existence, which means that the being has a starting point, unlike God, who has no beginning or end. The fact that God cannot create another God does not make God any weaker.

Those who try to make God greater by claiming that He can do those logically impossible things might sound good, but not true. God can, and He does the miraculous, but He does not do the logically impossible. It is true that God created the universe from nothing and cause the deaf to hear, the blind to see, the lame to walk, the dumb to talk, and the dead to live again. However, to claim that God does the logically impossible is to claim madness not miracle. God cannot make a square circle, because, by definition, a square is different in its description from a circle. Likewise, it is impossible for God to make a married bachelor, because by definition, a bachelor is an unmarried man. The only way the contradiction goes away is to change the meaning of the words, which is what Compatibilists promote to stay afloat.

Try to identify the contradiction in the Compatibilists' teaching. Listen carefully, because sometimes the contradiction might not be readily evident to the untrained ear. The more you know and understand truth, the more you will be able to identify that which is false. For example, unless someone already knows that a circle is different from a square, he might not really pick up on the contradiction. However, if the listener does know that, then it immediately becomes clear to him that ascribing that ability to God is not only a contradiction, but pure nonsense.

Since Compatibilists and hard Determinists believe that God has determined everything that comes to pass; and nothing happens apart from what He has decreed from all eternity, why do they still talk about God's intervention into the working and plan of salvation? Why use language like 'intervene', if what God has determined actually comes to pass? Are we to believe that God is preventing or stopping things He Himself has determined to happen? To intervene means to change, alter, or stop a result from happening. Is God changing in time, the things He has determined before time began? Doesn't that seem as if God is resisting and rejecting His own decree, and is therefore going against the manifestation of His declaration? Why does their teaching sound so confusing to me? If all events that happen in the world are definitely ordained by the Sovereign God, then why is He changing the course on which He has set the world?

Contradictions abound on the Compatibilists' system in many areas. Take for example, their constant proclamation that regeneration comes before someone places faith in God. We already dealt with this point and showed the biblical evidence that a person believes and then is given life. Here are a few reminders from Scripture. John 3:16 declares, those who believe will have eternal life; and John 1:11-12, those who receive Jesus by trusting in Him are given the right to become sons of God. We are told in John 20:31 that the Scriptures were written that people might believe, and in believing they might have life. The Apostle Paul says that we are raised with Him through faith (Colossians 2:12).

The reason I want to revisit their doctrine on this point is because it is another point of contradiction. Follow me closely on this. The Compatibilists claim that a person needs to be regenerated before he/she can believe, but their regeneration is described as something different from what the Bible calls regeneration. Since we covered regeneration earlier, I will only mention the fact that it means to be born again, or to be given a new life by the Holy Spirit. A person that is regenerated in the biblical sense is a person that is saved or born anew on the inside.

The regeneration of the Compatibilist only serves to make him/her aware and awake, because at that point he/she is still not saved. Compatibilists claim to agree that a person must believe to be saved. However, in their doctrine, they have a regenerated person who is not saved, because he/she is not yet a believer. It doesn't matter how close they want to put the time of the person's believing, it still does not change the fact that on their system, a person receives regeneration without salvation. They claim that the regenerated person receives a life, but it is not eternal life.

Since only those who have Christ have life (1 John 5:11-13), what kind of life is this that the Bible does not tell us about? And, from where does this life come? Their claim is the opposite of what Scripture teaches. The text says, "And this is the testimony: God has given us eternal life and this life is in His Son, whoever has the Son has life; whoever does not have the Son of God does not have life. I write these things to you who believe in the name of the Son of God so that you may know that you have eternal life."

The Apostles in Scripture cannot be any clearer. They all tell us that only those who believe have eternal life. Note that the Bible does not say that they get eternal life so that they believe; it says that they believe and then receive eternal life. Only those who have Christ through faith in Him, have eternal life. With this truth firmly planted, what kind of life are Compatibilists claiming that a person receives before he places faith in Christ?

It gets worse. If the person is "regenerated" so that person is made able to come "alive" and believe, is that person not made better than the non-elect, so that he can do the right thing? Although the Compatibilists insist that salvation comes only from God, and I do affirm that, do they not also secretly affirm that the un-regenerated "Elect," was made better before he believed, so that he could believe and receive the wonderful gift of God? Or, is it because they have not followed the logical implication which leads to that conclusion? If anyone would brag, would it not more likely be the one who was made better so that he could believe? I know they don't like the language I am using, but would it not be true that they are better because they are given "life"; that is, before eternal life? They are given eyes and a will to want God before they trusted in Jesus. So, would you not call that better?

I recently heard a preacher who is clearly driven by his Deterministic worldview say that those who are worried about the fact that their children might be numbered among the non-elect, have no reason to be concerned but they must only pray. Another member was worried that he might be rejected in the end if he was not one of the elect, even though he has been a professing believer for many years. He too was told by the Pastor that the fact that he has the heart-felt concern about his eternal destiny is proof that he is one of the elect. This was so shocking to hear because that does not line up with Determinism; and this preacher is one of the most famous Compatibilist in the world today.

The advice that was given to both persons is contradictory to the Determinists' / Compatibilists' doctrine. If the Pastor was speaking plainly, he would tell her that if her babies were not elected from before the foundation of the world, then they are going to hell, which was determined for them before they were born. That does not sound very caring, even though it would be true in their worldview. The member, who was told that he was one of the Elect because of the evidence of his concern about his final destination, was given false hope that does not come from the Determinists' system. On their system, no one knows for sure who the "Elect" are, and they cannot know until they stand before the Judge, Jesus.

When I watch the television and read books written by Determinists, I am convinced that they want to persuade persons through their preaching and teaching, that God has decreed everything that comes to pass before the foundation of the world. If God is the One who is leading them to teach Determinism to mature His Church over the world, why has He also determined the majority of His Elect to reject Compatibilism and hard Determinism? Is it because God does not want the majority of His Elect to mature in the faith and truth? If we who reject Determinism are hindering God's will by not accepting the Deterministic philosophy as true, it means that we have free will, which can impact what God wants for us.

Otherwise, it is because God wants those who do not accept Determinism to stay in their naïve and ignorant state which only leads to immaturity and a weak Christian life. If God has determined us to reject Determinism, they must not judge us as rebellious, less they find themselves rebelling against God, whose will it is for us to be rebellious if their doctrine is true.

If Determinists really believe that nothing comes to pass in the world apart from the will of God; then they should be consistent in their worldview. This means they should give praise to God for situations and events in the world where young children are raped and killed; when people are murdered mercilessly. I say this because Determinists insist that God causes every good and every evil that comes to pass. This they always seek to justify by pointing to the crucifixion. They claim that the crucifixion was the plan of God, and He caused evil men to do that great cruelty to His Son. If they want to be consistent with their philosophy, they need to praise God for the rapes and murders and all other evils in the same way they praise God for the crucifixion. I don't think that is something their doctrine will move them to celebrate.

One more problem with the Determinists' doctrine worth mentioning as it relates to the view that God from eternity past has ordained or decreed all things that come to pass. In the Bible, there are many situations where God changed what He said He was going to do and did something different. Exodus 32:14 says, "Then the LORD relented and did not bring on his people the disaster He has threatened." Jeremiah 18:8 says,

> And if that nation I warned repents of its evil, then I will relent and not inflict on it the disaster I had planned. And if at another time I announce that nation or kingdom is to be built up and planted, and if it does evil in my sight and does not obey me then I will reconsider the good I had intended to do for it.

We read the same truth in Jeremiah 26:13, where God made a decree, but He relented when the people repented. We see this repeatedly in Scripture; where God decreed a thing and then not bring to pass what He had told them He was going to do. The

Book of Jonah is a clear example of that. The people prayed and repented, and God showed them mercy (Jonah 3:10).

Determinists claim that they pray because it changes them. However, that is not the purpose for prayer in Scripture. People were taught by Jesus to pray to God, and it was not just about making them better. Prayer is primarily for God's divine intervention into the affairs of men. The model prayer given by Jesus in Matthew 6:9-13, presents different aspects of prayer. For example, there is praise and adoration. There is supplication and confession to ultimately get God's intervention, in which His will gets done on earth as it is done in heaven. In Determinism, does prayer change anything? In the Bible God changes things when people pray. In Jeremiah 26:19, the prophet Jeremiah sought the Lord, and the Lord did not bring disaster on the people like He had promised.

King Hezekiah fell sick and was told by the prophet Isaiah that he was going to die. Hezekiah then prayed to God and God changed that decree and gave Hezekiah fifteen more years after he prayed (2 Kings 20:1-6). It was not Hezekiah's powerful prayer that made the difference. It was his powerful God that made the difference when he prayed.

Questions to Contemplate/Discuss

a. What is Determinism?
b. Did God determine everything that happened in the world?

c. What is the evidence that everything is determined by God?
d. Does God's knowledge of an event cause it to come into being?
e. How can someone be responsible if his desires and actions were fixed by God?
f. How would you prove that Total Determinism is true?
g. Why would you say total Determinism is false?

CHAPTER 13

Love of God

13.1
God: The Lover

The main emphasis in the presentation of God by Determinists is that God is the Sovereign Ruler of the universe and therefore, He deserves our worship. The Bible, however, places emphasis in its revelation of God, as a lover. The essence therefore of who God is; is love. The Bible says,

> Dear friends, let us love one another, for love comes from God. Everyone who loves has been born of God and knows God. Whoever does not love, does not know God, because God is love. This is how God showed His love among us: He sent his one and only Son into the world that we might live through him" (1 John 4:7-9).

The emphasis that the Apostle John puts on God's essence is love. We need to make a distinction between who God is, and what He does. God is love. That is the essence of who He is. This was the very essence of God from all eternity. Let me make this plain; God loved, long before He was ruling. In other words, love was being expressed among the Father, Son (Word) and Holy Spirit, before the universe was created. Therefore, before God was Sovereign Ruler over anything or anyone, He loved. When there was no one or anything to rule over, because they did not yet exist; God was a loving Person.

Determinists need to be driven by the focus that the Bible puts on the nature or character of God. According to the text above, it is because of God's great love that He sent His Son, so that believing in Him we might have life eternal. John 3:14-18 describes for us how the loving God provides. He provided a Savior for the sins of the world because all have sinned. He promised that whoever looks to the Savior in faith will have eternal life. God informs us that, He did not send His Son into the world to condemn it, but to save the world through Christ. Everyone who refuses to believe is already condemned, but all those who believe will not be condemned but is passed from death to life. We will now look at how the Bible describes the love of God' We are convinced that it does not resemble what the Compatibilist proclaim or would like God's love to be.

Compatibilists describe the Love of God in a very strange way; one that in no way fits the description of the God of the Bible. First, they constantly declare that people should be amazed that God would choose to save even one person. They promote that idea because of their view on total depravity. I affirm the truth that mankind is so depraved that there is no way mankind could do any good to save themselves. Mankind has nothing within them that caused God to seek after them to save them. However, the Good News of the Bible is not that God saw us looking good and pleasing in His sight, and so He came to rescue us. Nor does it say that human beings were not so bad, therefore God came to rescue them.

The picture that the Scriptures give of the fall and separation of mankind between them and their God, is that mankind was lost and God had to find them. Mankind was naked, and God had to clothe them. Mankind was dead, (spiritually separated from God) and God made a promise to send a Redeemer, who is Christ.

When I look at the God of the Bible, and compare Him with what is described by the Compatibilist, I am convinced that they are not describing the God of the Bible. The God of the Bible does not seem to be the type of person who would leave the individual who is sinking in the sea to drown. Their idea that shows God to be loving and gracious because He saves only one out of the hundred individuals who were drowning is a misrepresentation of God and of the biblical description of love.

Picture a man called John watching a hundred people drowning, and then going out and saving only one. Would you think that the individual is caring for doing that? Yes! You would. On the other hand, what if he said to you that he could actually rescue all of the people who were drowning, but he only wanted to save one? Would you not think that he was wicked? The fact that he/she was not obligated to saving any of them would not stop you from thinking that he is wicked for not saving more of them, since he was able to save all of them. The loving God of the Bible would go back out in the ocean to rescue even one, if the other ninety-nine were safe on the shore. This is the picture we get from Scripture (Luke 15:4).

Furthermore, I would be quite surprised if God would pass the sinner without seeking to rescue him/her. Jesus, like the Good Samaritan in the parable of Luke 10:25-37, is the one who does not pass by the needy. The Samaritan stopped to help, not because he had to, but because he wanted to. The Samaritan chose to show kindness, not because the person deserved it, but because the Samaritan is kind. Jesus Christ came and died for us sinners, not because we deserved it, but because He loves us (John 3:16). If some people were chosen for damnation from before the creation, it would be better if they were not born. According to Determinism, God did not take anything into consideration when He chose people for salvation. This means that God could have chosen more people or everyone for salvation, since it has nothing to do with their sin or their faith in God. Let me explain. In Determinism, a person goes to Hell not because of any sin he has committed, but because God decreed it to be so before the world was created. Determinists claim that God gave some people life, even before they trusted Christ for eternal life.

13.2
Is this Love?

If I believe what the Bible says in 1 Corinthians 13:1-7, then I can be assured that God's love seeks what is best for the person. According to the Apostle Paul, love is not just the giving of food, clothe, or health to live a long life. A person can have great faith and even give great gifts to those who are poor and still not have love. It means, therefore, that these things in and of themselves are not defined as love. This goes to show that someone can give without truly loving; but the person that truly loves cannot, but give. This is why we are told that God gave. He gave more than just rain and food to the just and the unjust, because those things in and of themselves do not mean love.

According to McQuilkin (1995), there are two elements in the biblical concept of love. Love is a noun that may indicate feelings, and it is also a verb that emphasizes doing. This fact is both true for God and man (p. 4). McQuilkin (1995), states that in the Bible the emphasis of demonstrating love goes beyond our feelings. This is so true because we can feel one way, but act in another way which is contrary to how we feel. If one has compassion, then it must show. God so loved the world that He gave!

The contrast I am making here is that although Determinists insist that God loves the "non-elect", because He gives him food, clothe and rain, falls short of a true description of love in the Bible. 1 John 4:8 tells us that God is love. This is the very essence and nature of God. If God is only interested in giving the 'non-elect' rain and food and clothe what does that profit since his soul has been designated for hell? Giving the non- elect good things for this life, while banning him from receiving eternal life, is no love at all. For what does it profit a man if he gains the whole world and to lose his soul? What can a man give in exchange for his soul? (Mark 8:36-37, KJV).

Jesus has demonstrated His love and grace to strangers. He prayed while He was on the cross that His father would show mercy to those who nailed Him to the cross (Luke 23:34). We do not have to guess about the kind of Person the Father is, because Jesus tells us that when we see Him, we see what the Father is like. We are able to know the Father by looking at the life of His Son (John 14:7-9). Jesus is the express image of the Father, according to Hebrews 1:1. Therefore, whatever the Father is was demonstrated in the life of His Son. Jesus came to earth that He might reveal the Heavenly Father to us. No man has seen the Father, but His Only Begotten Son has revealed Him (John 1:18). If Jesus was so moved to rescue the perishing and to care for the dying, then we can be sure what the Father thinks, because Jesus is just like His Father.

In my country Jamaica, a popular adage goes, "So di Fada, so di Son" (the Son is like the Father). This truth is clearly taught in Scripture, and it means that who the Father is, has been manifested in the life of His Son. So while you are thinking about God as a Great Ruler, remember that He was a Great Lover first. God is not focused on the free will of mankind, but He wants men to truly love Him. This can only happen if mankind is really free.

Questions to Contemplate/Discuss

a. Give a description of Love
b. In what way does God love everyone?
c. In what way is the love of God in the Bible different from in Determinism?

CHAPTER 14:
Amazing Grace

We have been on a rough journey through the components of salvation. We have also contended with Determinism as we tackled Compatibilism. We have exposed the hidden meanings in their worldview, and proven it to be contradictory to the Scripture. Therefore, Compatibilism is not a good representation of the love of God and the freedom that is revealed in the Bible. Now that we have come to the final chapter of the book, we want to see what the Bible says about grace. Grace plays a very significant role in the salvation of the believer, and, also for the sustenance of every human being. All that Christians have, all that they are, and all that they will receive or become in eternity is because of the grace of God.

14. 1
What is Grace?

The word grace plays a significant role in the Apostle Paul's theology because he considers grace to be the means by which we receive the kindness of God. It is God's unmerited favor given to us human beings. We could not earn God's grace, nor do we deserve it.

God has always been loving and kind, and that kindness was displayed on the cross, which is the ultimate demonstration of God's grace to us. After mankind fell in the Garden of Eden, it came to pass that God gave His laws through Moses, that would serve as a schoolmaster in showing us our need for a Savior and leading us to Christ (Galatians 3:24). The Law was not given so that man would be saved by it, because if obeying the Law could take away sin, then Christ would have died in vain (Galatians 2:21). The writer of Hebrews says that the blood of bulls and goats and ceremonial washings and sacrifices were only external regulations applying until the new order in Christ comes (Hebrews 9:10). Hebrews 10:1 says that "It is impossible for the blood of bulls and goats to take away sins."

This is why Jesus is the essence of grace. He is the intrinsic nature and indispensable quality that is absolutely necessary for us to benefit from the grace of God. It was the sacrifice of Christ that gives hope to all who trust in God. This is true of Old and New Testament Saints alike. Every person's salvation is hinged on the resurrection of Jesus Christ. The Saints in the Old Testament looked forward to the Redeemer of Mankind, who is Christ. For there is no other Name under heaven given to mankind by which we must be saved, for salvation is found in no one else (Acts 4:12).

We read in Hebrews 10:8-10, which says,

> Sacrifices and offerings, burnt offerings and sin offerings you did not desire, nor were you pleased with them, though they were offered in accordance with the law. Then He said, 'Here I am, I have come to do your will; He sets aside the first to establish the second, and by that will, we have been made holy through the sacrifice of the body of Jesus Christ once for all.'

The Apostle John also informs us that the Law was given by Moses, but grace and truth came by Jesus Christ (John 1:17).

This does not mean that no one received grace before Jesus came to earth, but it does mean that the essence and fullness of God's grace came in Christ. The Apostle John testified that he has seen the manifestation of the Son of God who came in flesh and dwelt among men; and He is full of grace and truth (John 1:14).

14.2
The Good News of Grace

The Apostle Paul made it clear that his only purpose for living was to finish the race and complete the task that was given to him by Jesus Christ. This most important task according to him, is to testify or proclaim the Gospel of God's grace (Acts 20:24). I want to join the Apostle Paul in this most honorable obligation of preaching the Good News of God's grace.

14.3
Grace to Enter

God, the All-Sufficient and All-Loving One has made it possible for persons to enter into His grace, by faith in Jesus Christ. Romans 5:1-2 says, "Therefore, since we have been justified by faith, we have peace with God through our Lord Jesus Christ, through whom we have gained access by faith into His grace in which we now stand. And we boast in the hope of the glory of God." We were able to enter this privileged position or place of grace by trusting in Jesus Christ. It is by grace through faith we enter into righteousness and eternal life.

There is a beautiful passage of Scripture about God's grace to us in 2 Corinthians 8:9. It says, "For you know the grace of our Lord Jesus Christ, that though He was rich yet for your sakes He became Poor, so that you through His poverty might become rich." Christ gives us righteousness and riches to cover our rags and wretchedness when we place our trust in Him. In Ephesians 1:6-8, the Apostle Paul tells us that God has lavished on us His glorious grace through Christ in whom we have redemption and forgiveness of sins through His blood. Oh, what an amazing grace. Hallelujah!

15.4
Grace to Enable

God is loving and kind, but He does not just grace us because He is gracious; He has a purpose for giving grace. Let us look at some of the purposes for God's grace in our lives. God wants us to live by grace through faith in the same way that we were saved by grace through faith. As we mentioned at the beginning of this chapter, grace is God's unmerited favor to us. It is the divine enablement which assists us in accomplishing the task God has given us to do. Please note, that we cannot earn, nor do we deserve God's grace, but it is given to us freely by His own love. It is a special empowerment which is provided by God to do the work to which we are called. Therefore, God did not only give us grace for salvation, He also gave us grace for service to Him. The Apostle Paul tells us that through Jesus they received grace and apostleship to call all the Gentiles to the obedience that comes from faith in His name (Romans 1:5).

The Lord has given us all that we need for life and godliness through our knowledge of Him who called us by His own glory and goodness (2 Peter 1:3). It is in Him we live and move and have our existence (Acts 17:28). This means that even the next breath I take comes from God, and I can't live without Him. If we are going to live a fruitful life that is honoring to God, we must be obedient to the Spirit, so that we do not gratify the desires of the flesh (Galatians 5:16). This means to keep in line or in step with what God tells you to do. Unless we abide in Him and allow His Word to abide in us, we will not bear fruit. However, if we keep in step with the Spirit, we will bear much fruit. God is at work in us to desire and to do, that which pleases Him (Philippians 2:13). He is constantly speaking to our conscience and spirit to walk in His Will.

You do not need to worry about having what you need to live a good Christian life, because "God is able to make all grace abound to you so that you always have all sufficiency in all things, may abound to every good work" (2 Corinthians 9:8). The Lord supplies what we need. He sustains us and strengthens us when we are growing weary. Therefore, the Lord invites us to come boldly unto the throne of grace where we can find grace to help in times of need (Hebrews 4:16). Notice that grace is in store; ready and waiting for us to come to God for help. Make sure that while you come to His throne boldly and confidently, you don't come proudly, and insincerely.

14.5
Don't take Grace for Granted

The Apostle Paul challenged believers to be grateful for God's Amazing Grace, and not take grace for granted. Romans 5:20 says, that where sin increased, grace increased even more. This, however, does not give us license to sin more, so that we can get more grace. The Apostle Paul tells us that no believer should even be thinking like that, because we have died to sin and should no longer live in sin (Romans 6:1-2). We are given grace in order that we might live as people who were set free from sin, and not to become entangled with the bondage of sin again. The grace that God brings to our lives is to enable us to live in a manner that pleases Him.

Here is a beautiful picture of the role of grace in a life of submission to God. Titus 2:11-12 says, "For the grace of God has appeared that offers salvation to all people. It teaches us to say 'no' to ungodliness and worldly passions; and to live self-controlled, upright, and godly lives in this present age." This is a clear declaration that grace comes to our lives that we might live right in God's sight.

Now that we have been washed by the blood of Christ and received of the Father's glorious grace, we must get rid of the works of the flesh, such as malice, deceit, hypocrisy, envy, and slander; and seek the Word of God that we might grow in our salvation to spiritual maturity (1 Peter 2:1-2). The Apostle Peter says that since we have tasted the Lord's goodness and grace, it is fitting that we live for Him. Romans 12:1-2, tells us that in the light of God's mercies to us, we should present ourselves to God and do not be conformed to the world system, but rather be transformed by renewing our minds with the word of God. We can and we should grow in grace and the knowledge of Christ (2 Peter 3:18).

14. 6
Grace to Engage

As we seek to impact the world in a positive way for Christ, we must rely on God's grace to engage with life's challenges and accomplish the task that we are left here to do. Grace is sufficient for every work to which the believer is called. The Apostle Paul in 2 Corinthians 1:12 says, that he and his fellow servants of Christ were able to conduct themselves with integrity through the Grace of God, and not through worldly wisdom. The wisdom that guided their interactions with people was from above, and not earthly.

We are encouraged to be wise in the way we deal with the unsaved. We are also to make the most of every opportunity that we have to impact people for Christ. Colossians 4:6 says, "Let your conversation be always full of grace, seasoned with salt, so that you may know how to answer everyone." We must be careful that we do not put a stumbling block in the path of people, and turn them away from Christ and salvation. Jesus says that we are salt and light (Matthew 5:13-16). We are encouraged and commanded by Jesus to let our light shine. This means that we should let our life shine and be a blessing to those around us in this dark world. We might be the only representation that people will see and come to know the love of Jesus.

The key to engage with others in a way that pleases God is not just to give (of) ourselves; but to give (up) ourselves. God graced the Macedonian churches which were going through severe trials, and they were generous in giving to people who were less fortunate. They were struggling financially but they gave much out of their little, so that they could be a blessing to others. Most persons would refuse to give or help in that state of poverty.

However, the reason they were able to give to the Apostles, was because they gave themselves to God first. Here is a picture of persons who were surrendered to God. The Macedonians recognized that all that they are, and all that they have belong to God. So, when they gave up themselves to God, it became easier to give of themselves to the need that was present (2

Corinthians 8:1-5). Let us, therefore, give up ourselves for the total leading of the Spirit of God, so that we might be effective witnesses for Him.

14. 7
Grace to Endure

God gives us grace to endure the difficulties in life, regardless of the source of the problems we are facing. The Apostle Paul had a very serious problem which he refers to as a "thorn in the flesh." No one knows what exactly his "thorn in the flesh" was, and that might be to our benefit, because we might have other "thorns" that do not look like the Apostle Paul's, but we need the same response as he did. Paul mentions the fact that the devil tormented him through this 'thorn in the flesh'. He also tells us that he went to the Lord three times and pleaded for God to remove the thorn. This is the Lord's response: "My grace is sufficient for you, for my power is made perfect in weakness" (2 Corinthians 12:9).

When we get a good perspective of what God's grace is able to help us to accomplish, it lifts our confidence and strengthens our faith in God. Notice that at first, the Apostle Paul was crying out to God to remove the problem. However, when he got heavenly insight, his perspective changed, and he was able to rejoice in spite of the problem. Note that God did not remove Paul's problem in order to increase his strength. It was then that Paul recognized that when he was weak in his own strength, he was able to rest and rejoiced in the power of God. We too need to remember that when we have everything under control, we usually trust in ourselves, our money, our family, and our friends. The Apostle Paul had to just let go off his own will and way, and trust in God who is his strength.

14.8
Grace to End Well

The last passage of Scripture we want to look at in our study of grace-living is 2 Timothy 4:6-8, which says, "For I am already being poured out like a drink offering, and the time for my departure is near. I have fought a good fight, I have finished the race, I have kept the faith. Now there is in store for me the crown of righteousness, which the Lord, the righteous Judge, will award me on that day, and not only me, but also to all who have longed for his appearing."

The Apostle Paul was nearing death, but he was looking forward to meeting Christ with great anticipation, because he knew that he completed the task that the Lord had given him to do. The fact that he ran well, he was quite sure that the Judge of all the earth will reward him for his faithful service. The key to being rewarded and hearing well done from God for your service here on earth, is to make sure that your motives are good, and your service is faithful to God. It is not about the success of your ministry, rather, it is about your faithful commitment and witness for God. So, let us go out into the world to make disciples for Christ, and do all to the glory of God.

Questions to Contemplate/Discuss

a. What is Grace?
b. Does everyone receive grace from God?
c. Is grace and mercy the same thing?
d. How can we live a life led by grace?
e. What can we do so that we don't take grace for granted?

Conclusion

My desire for those who read this book is that they will all finish well; that they will develop the skills and the right attitude to contend for the faith. For Christians, this means that we need to know, and do what the Lord commands us to do, which is primarily to be an extension and an example of Christ's love to people. We need to be mindful that we must give an account for the time, talents and treasures that God has given us to use for His glory in this earth.

Let us, therefore, be yielded to Christ and not treat Him like the Church in Revelation 3:20, who continued to have church service, but Jesus was left outside knocking on the door for someone, anyone to let Him in. Let us not try to do the work of the Lord without the Lord of the work. Time is going by quickly, let us not waste more time. After all has been said and done, the whole duty of mankind is to fear God and to obey His Word (Ecclesiastes 12:13). There is an urgent call to every believer to go and tell that the Lord is good. There is also an urgent call to the unsaved to come and taste that the Lord is good.

I pray that the unsaved will recognize that tomorrow is not promised to anyone, that they will not harden their hearts when they hear the Gospel. I pray that they will not allow themselves to be tricked by the devil to think that they are not so bad, or that they might think that they have more time to decide. Now is the accepted time. Today is the day of salvation. Please do not try to be rich in this world and be poor toward God.

Let me close with this benediction from 2 Corinthians 13:14. "May the grace of the Lord Jesus Christ, and the love of God, and the fellowship of the Holy Spirit be with you all." Amen.

About the Author

Garfield Robinson communicates the Scripture in a clear and concise manner, filled with conviction. His passion is teaching people how to understand the Scripture, and to improve their spiritual intimacy with God. He has a gift of using simple and common examples to communicate complex truths. He has been a football player and a coach for many years, and he has applied some of his coaching techniques in his ministry. This he often does by creating a picture of what is happening in the text.

He is convinced that people have questions, and they need someone to give some satisfying answers. He is confident that the Bible has relevant answers to help people today. This is the thesis of this dynamic book by this gifted Bible teacher and disciple maker.

References

Allen, David. 2016.*The extent of the atonement. A historical critical review.* B and H. Nashville Academic.

Duvall, Scott. J and J. Hays, Daniel. 2005. *Grasping God's Word, 2nd Edition.* Zondervan Grand Rapids.

Evans, Tony. 1999. *Who is this king of glory?* Moody press.

_____. *The kingdom agenda.* Moody Publishers

Flowers, Leighton. 2017. *The potter's promise: A biblical defense of traditional soteriology.* Trinity Academic.

Geisler, Norman. 2001. *Chosen but Free.* 2nd Edition, Bethany House.

Geisler, Norman and Bocchino, Peter. 2001. *Unshakable Foundations.* Bethany House.

Grudem, Wayne. 1994. *Systematic Theology: An introduction to Biblical Doctrine*. Zondervan Publishers

Lennox, John C. 2017. *Determined to believe? The sovereignty of God, freedom faith and human responsibility*. Grand Rapids: Zondervan

McQuilkin, Robertson. 1995. *Introduction to Biblical ethics: 2nd edition* Tyndale House Publishers,

Moreland, J. P. Scaling.1987. *The secular city*. Baker Books.

Rogers, Ronnie W. 2019. *Does God love some, or all? Comparing biblical extensivism and Calvinism's exclusivism*. WIPF and Stock.

Sproul, R. C. 1986. *Chosen by God*. Tyndale House Publishers.

Made in the USA
Columbia, SC
28 July 2022